Wakefield Press

COAST TO COAST

Nick Petrucco is happily married to Bec and they have three amazing kids, Indy, Maggie and Gus. After several years on the Mornington Peninsula and a couple in Penang, Malaysia, Nick and his family returned to Adelaide in late 2014.

Nick and Bec shared the responsibility of leading Beyond Synergy – a family foundation dedicated to improving the health, safety and education of children around the world. With support of family and friends, Beyond Synergy funded the rebuilding of a children's home in India, established women's empowerment programs in India, and provided operational funds for a young girls' home in Cambodia; schools in Afghanistan and Kenya were also funded as well as an annual nutrition program for homeless children in Melbourne. More recently, Nick and his family walked the breadth of southern India, funding multiple projects for kids along the way.

Nick has always loved to write as a way of sharing what he thinks and feels with people he cares about. *Coast to Coast* is Nick's first attempt at sharing those words with a broader audience.

Coast to Coast

A Family Walk Across India

Nick Petrucco

Wakefield Press
16 Rose Street
Mile End
South Australia 5031
www.wakefieldpress.com.au

First published 2016

Edited by Molly Jureidini, Wakefield Press
Cover designed by Liz Nicholson, designBITE
Text designed and typeset by Wakefield Press
Printed in Australia by Griffin Press, Adelaide

National Library of Australia Cataloguing-in-Publication entry

Creator:	Petrucco, Nick, author.
Title:	Coast to coast: a family walk across India / Nick Petrucco.
ISBN:	978 1 74305 424 6 (paperback).
Subjects:	Petrucco, Nick – Family.
	ChildFund Australia.
	Fund raisers (Persons) – India – Anecdotes.
	Fund raising – India.
	Walking – India.
	India – Description and travel.
Dewey Number:	361.70681

Wakefield Press thanks Coriole Vineyards for their continued support.

For my family,

who are truly my inspiration. You remind me every day that while I may not be able to do everything I surely can do something. You have always encouraged me to follow my dreams no matter how crazy they might seem!

Also to my good mate Tim. I hope that every day of my life is a reflection of the respect I have for you and yours. You left us way too early, my friend.

Part proceeds from the sale of *Coast to Coast* will be donated to ChildFund Australia to support their work around the world with children and their communities to create lasting and meaningful change.

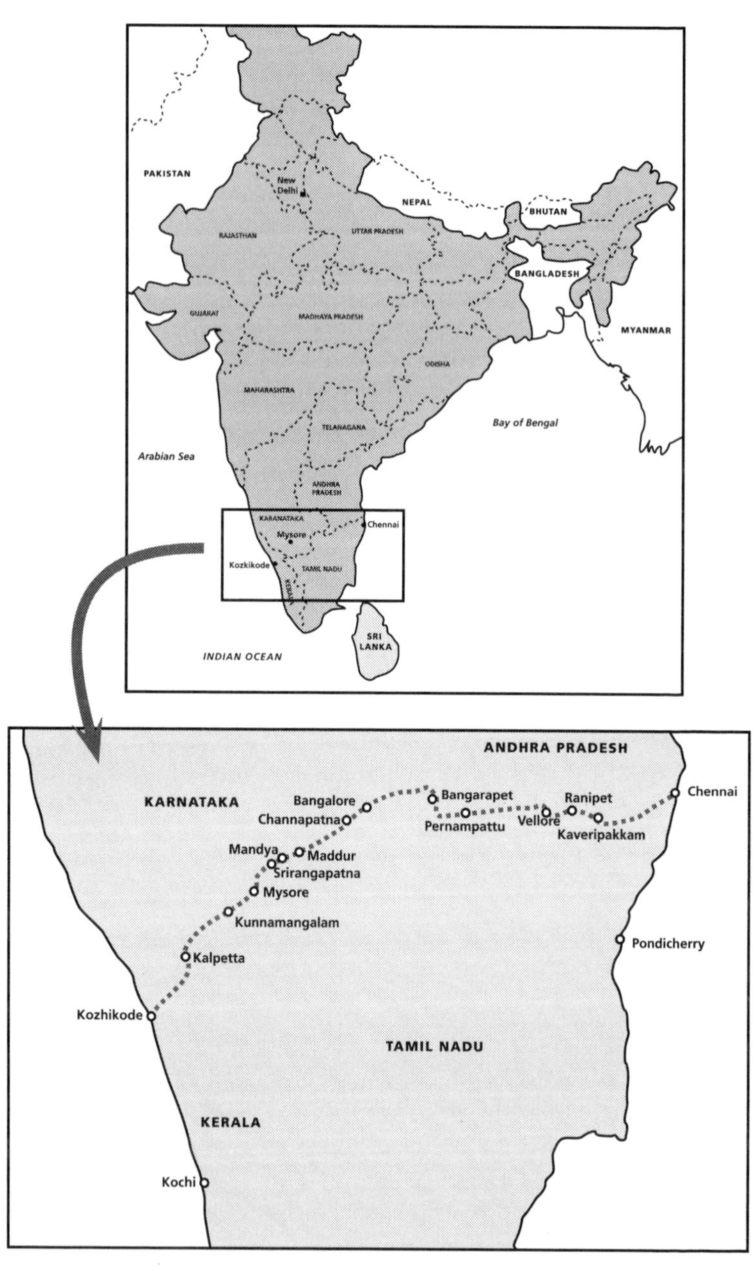
PAKISTAN
New Delhi
NEPAL
BHUTAN
RAJASTHAN
UTTAR PRADESH
BANGLADESH
GUJARAT
MADHAYA PRADESH
MYANMAR
ODISHA
MAHARASHTRA
TELANAGANA
Bay of Bengal
Arabian Sea
ANDHRA PRADESH
KARANATAKA
Chennai
Mysore
Kozkikode
TAMIL NADU
SRI LANKA
INDIAN OCEAN
ANDHRA PRADESH
KARNATAKA
Bangalore
Bangarapet
Ranipet
Chennai
Channapatna
Pernampattu
Vellore
Kaveripakkam
Mandya
Maddur
Srirangapatna
Mysore
Kunnamangalam
Pondicherry
Kalpetta
Kozhikode
TAMIL NADU
KERALA
Kochi

Contents

Introduction

For so many reasons this book nearly failed to be written. After the year away, I returned to working full-time running a business, trying to be a good husband and a father of three growing kids, managing our foundation and its many projects, and trying to keep fit and healthy. You know what it's like. But as is sometimes the case, I couldn't move forward without sharing my experience with others, and eventually I was able to find the space and time I needed to stop and capture our amazing family adventure.

I wanted to write this book for all of the people like me who have desperately tried to find the motivation to get through just one more day at work. Those who have thought there must be more to life, who questioned the notion that life is only about having a family, a house, and a job where you work long hours. That this somehow means that you have made it, and your life is now supposed to be complete. I remember the time when I sat and asked myself, 'What is wrong with me? Why am I not feeling the happiness and satisfaction I was expecting?' This book is a way of sharing our struggle to make our lives meaningful and to focus on what really matters to us: quality time together as a family, encouraging a spirit of adventure, and working to make a difference in the lives of kids.

You will be introduced to my family – my wife Bec, our three kids India, Maggie and Gus, my parents Jenny and Nick (yes, another Nick), my sister Kate and her two kids Alice and Max. We are not an adventurous family. I am not well equipped with outdoor skills. Our idea of a family adventure is a non-powered campsite for our caravan. We do not consider ourselves wealthy, but would probably be classified as middle class. At the time of the walk we were both nearing forty years of age, we had a home with seventy-five per cent of the value mortgaged to the bank, we had two cars – one with a large lease – and we had a little superannuation saved for our retirement. We were struggling to work out how to balance providing our kids with a good education with the desire to have the life that Bec and I had always wanted to lead. When we decided to do the walk, we drew on our mortgage and used the small savings we had. In the end we had to sell our caravan to fund the additional expenses of the trip, as everything cost more than we had expected. This is not about crying poor. We are rich in so many ways as a result of the trip. I say this for that inevitable moment when you might think that you couldn't do something like this, that we were rich and had the time to go on an adventure. The reality is that we didn't really have the money for the trip – or the time – but we made it work, and we have been grateful ever since. Grateful we had the courage to make this adventure a priority over all of the everyday stuff that usually wins.

If you can relate to this then I hope this book becomes a catalyst for you. We may have walked across India but, as you will discover, the real journey was so much more than that.

PART ONE

Australia

1 We Made It!

It was a hot, dusty and dry day, weather we had grown accustomed to. Sitting at the feet of a Mahatma Gandhi statue on a paved area adjacent to Marina Beach in Chennai, East India, I took a moment to try to absorb the enormity of what we had achieved, reflect on the people we had met, the many adventures we had experienced, and all of the highs and lows that an epic journey brings. Our walk had not let us down. We had traversed over 1000 kilometres from the west to the east coast of India – over 600 of these we walked as a family. As I drew in a deep breath, my gaze turned toward the beach and the sand stretching as far as the eye could see. The kids decided that sitting by a statue of an old man they didn't know just wasn't enough for them, so they started running for the water as only kids can on a hot day. Their little legs had carried them many hundreds of kilometres, yet far from exhausted, they were elated with their accomplishment. Or was it relief that this was over, and they could once again go back to sleeping in and enjoying what was left of their holidays? Either way, they had been fuelled to sprint to the finish line – and the waves rolling in on the Marina Beach shoreline.

2 The Seed Forms

An eternity ago we were staying in the Barwon Heads Caravan Park on the Bellarine Peninsula in Victoria. It was a mild morning in the September school holidays; the sun was shining but the air was crisp. We had just had a difficult and disappointing trip to Robe in South Australia visiting with family. On the way back we sensibly decided to spend a few days with our kids in Barwon Heads, one of those special little seaside towns that gets into your system. In our caravan and only metres from the ocean, we found shelter and space among the tea-trees of the park. We were in desperate need of inspiration. I could feel the darkness of depression creeping into my psyche once again, and I was determined not to let it return. Not after all we had sacrificed in recent years. But I was feeling flat and out of answers. I started reading a book focused on living life to the full, and finding a sense of purpose among the chaos of modern life. Reading can present a fresh perspective, and I saw this as a sign that I was ready to change. The book posed two critical questions for me, catalysts for a life-changing experience. What contribution do you want to make to this world? And what is it that you do that you could turn from ordinary to extraordinary? I started to think. What would our contribution be, or our something extraordinary?

3 Why India?

To understand why we connected to India I need to take you back to a couple of key periods in our lives. The first occurred on New Year's Day in 1996. I had travelled from Manchester to Mumbai en route to Chennai. I was a student travelling overseas for the first time, and about to spend four months in rural southern India, working as a student at a health and social affairs unit. Bec, who was then my girlfriend, was to join me midway through my placement, and spend some time in the hospital there to broaden her nursing experience.

For some, India is the last place they would want to go to and I can understand why. But sometimes a place gets into your soul and becomes a part of you. I never really had a yearning to travel when I was younger. When I was nineteen my parents offered to take me to Bali, but feeling a mix of fear and uncertainty I declined their offer. At university six years later I was absolutely inspired by a professor with a passion for social justice. He encouraged me to think broadly about my education, and before I knew it, I was planning my first trip overseas.

Landing in India was an absolute assault on the senses, as anyone who has been to India will tell you – the heat, smells and poverty, the rubbish and masses of people were overwhelming. For the first couple of weeks I pretty much locked myself in my room. I was ill and yearned to be home with Bec and my family. Gradually I found the courage to venture out into the streets and experience India. My fear slowly dissipated, and I had the experience of a lifetime. It was a challenge but also an incredible opportunity to discover more about myself, the world and my relationship with Bec.

My special memories of that early trip to India are many. I visited a HIV/AIDS clinic in Chennai and there met a young man, Boskarana. We were heading out by train to visit one of the local villages. I was distracted, and paying little attention to Boska, my host – a quiet and shy Indian man, who was a social worker for the clinic. As we went along, Boska started to share his story with me. He was from a village and travelled to the city for work, which he was enjoying. Boska was one of the 167 million Dalits, the so-called 'untouchables' who fall outside the caste system and face discrimination at every level of Indian society. He told me about his family. His brother had recently been murdered for no reason other than his caste, and Boska was now required to return home to look after his family. He believed that in all likelihood he too would be murdered upon his return home, but it was his duty to do so. It was a moment I will never forget. Here was a man about my age but with a very different life. I haven't heard from Boska since and often wonder what happened to him.

On another day I went for a walk around the beach in Chennai, and stumbled upon a slum not far from where I was staying. I caught the eyes of a couple of kids who were playing together as I approached. Before I knew it I was surrounded by a large group of local children and led into a makeshift classroom nearby. The room was about as big as our laundry, with thatched walls and a basic galvanised roof. There I sat looking at these beautiful kids; not being able to connect through language we communicated through smiles and gestures. Before we knew it we were singing songs together and dancing. Anyone who knows me knows that this is a big deal. I don't dance!

After several weeks in the city I headed to the country for my three-month placement at the Rural Unit for Health and Social Affairs (RUHSA). Here Bec joined me to share the challenge of growth and learning. We had a small room, a cold shower and were fifty metres from a railway line with very loud trains going past at all hours of the night. I was to work with a group of elderly Indian widows offering health care in the local villages, while Bec volunteered as a nurse. On my first day I showed up to work in forty-degree heat wearing shorts and was sent home to put on long pants and a shirt. Welcome to India!

There were many challenges for Bec and the medical staff at the clinic, but one day was particularly hard. She had been observing a difficult birth, a baby born far too early with no hope of survival. Once delivered, she was placed on a gurney for her first and final few breaths. No one held her. Bec moved over to take her hand as the life slowly drifted out of her little body.

One of the delights of our rural stay was the nights we spent on the roof of our dorm. Every night we would head up and look up at the beautiful starry sky, spectacularly bright in the absence of streetlights, debrief about our experiences of the day and ponder what it all meant. I'm not sure if we came up with any answers but we enjoyed the questions.

After several months we befriended a family. Paul owned the local store, and together with his wife, brother and four children, supplied tea, coffee, food and general supplies to the health unit staff. Bec and I became very close to Paul's family and in particular his children Subashini and Christopher. Many nights we would wander over for a cup of tea or coffee and talk with the kids. Christopher would often volunteer to take me on the back of his motorcycle to the local town for supplies, and Subashini and Bec would discuss her goal of one day becoming a nurse, which we are very proud to say she later achieved.

By the end of the four months and a diet of rice and the watery vegetable gravy known as samba, Bec and I were ready to return home. There were so many wonderful memories for first time travellers to India. But it was not all awe and wonder as I wrestled with Indian bureaucracy and my work failed to make an impact. This was a harsh awakening for an idealist student who thought he could change the world. Bec and I got engaged and vowed that if we ever had a daughter she would be called India, after our time there together. At that time we didn't expect we would ever head back. We had our experience, and it was time to return to our 'normal' life far away from the challenges India had presented. I ended up finishing my social work course and securing a senior management position in a bank, and our life headed on a very different trajectory.

4 India Calling Again

Fast-forward nine years to 2005. Bec and I were married with two beautiful children – our first named India. I had built a career in business and hadn't thought of India (the country) for many years. I had gained a lot of weight. I was making more money than I had ever dreamed of, and we were doing a good job spending it on a range of consumables – at the time it seemed like we couldn't live without them. We were a long way from those two young idealistic people living in India, and seemed to have lost any sense of balance or meaning.

One day I was sitting in a car park on Port Road in Adelaide, having just had some lunch (no, not anything healthy) and I couldn't drive back to work for my afternoon appointments. I wasn't sure what was going on. My mind and body felt numb. I couldn't face another day of working, and I didn't know where to turn. I just sat there. Throughout my life I had surpassed my own expectations. I had achieved every goal I had ever set for myself in terms of work and family. I owned all that I wanted or needed. Why was I so unhappy? It didn't make sense. Was this all that life had to offer? A house, cars, going to work, and living a kind of lukewarm, melancholic, groundhog day. Years before, as I drove to work each day, I would stop at a traffic light opposite a used Volkswagen car yard and a couple of old Kombi vans. Therein was my dream. I yearned for the freedom to leave behind all of my day-to-day issues and replace them with adventure. As I sat frozen in the car park I realised I had forgotten how to dream. Something had to change, but how?

I started to think again of India. I realised that while I had been busy building a life, I had lost connection with my soul, sense of purpose, and spirit of living. I rang a good friend working in Bangkok, and told her I was thinking it was time to return to India. She said she had a colleague who knew of an orphanage there that needed help. I then rang my old university professor, who, luck would have it, was about to go to India, and wanted me to help him run a social work conference at the rural health unit I had studied at in 1996. Bec urged me to go. She knew I wasn't in a good place and didn't know how to help. Three phone calls later I was on my way back to India, shit scared, and very far out of my comfort zone.

5 Learning to Make a Difference

Quite by chance in a country the size of India, the orphanage was near where I was staying, so I stopped in for a visit – one that would change my life. The home was situated in the outer suburbs of Ambattur, a major municipality in the Tiruvallur district in Chennai. As we drove through the streets, I was filled with a nervous excitement – something I hadn't felt for a long time. We left behind the main streets and wound our way through a series of labyrinthine narrow streets and alleys filled with small shops, dodging the street dogs, the cows, and the people, who were always going somewhere with a sense of purpose. Eventually we arrived. On the left side of the street was a small run-down school and across the narrow road on the right I could see a half-finished, three-storey building that looked closer to being demolished than built. As I stepped out of the car I could feel a buzz in the air and the occasional voice of a child, then two and three, and eventually a symphony of excited squeals and commotion. I walked into the derelict building, and saw fifty beautiful children sitting cross-legged on the floor awaiting my arrival, boys on my right and girls on my left. As anyone who has visited a children's home like this would know, it is a mixture of raw and powerful emotions. You are hit by the squalid living conditions and, in contrast, the children's beauty, courage and resilience. Only days before I had been sitting in my comfortable home playing with my girls. It now felt like a palace.

Many traditional songs and dances were performed as part of my welcome. It was quite the production. But the most moving part of my visit was to sit and listen to the children, who smiled from ear to ear as they told their stories. They shared with me how fortunate they felt to be cared for at the home. As a father of two (at the time), I knew of all the love, support, possessions and comfort my girls enjoyed in Australia, and when contrasted to what these children had, it strongly put into perspective what life was about. This moment forever changed the way I viewed the world.

After meeting the children I was given the privilege of reading their life stories, which were recorded once they arrived at the home. Page after page revealed horrifying experiences that no child should ever have to endure.

Children were brought to the home by social workers or police mostly due to the death, illness or poverty. Some were brought when their parents were imprisoned. Precious, a child with a severe disability, was left to die in a rubbish bin before being found and brought in. I began to understand why they felt so lucky to have a life of relative comfort, love and care.

I was shown through the partly renovated building, which was designed to accommodate for the growing number of children. The renovations were being completed little by little as the owners could afford it, and at the time of my visit funds weren't available and work had stalled. This meant that all of the children were forced to sleep together on the floor in one small room; there was no place for the sick or their carers. Within the room each child had a small hole in the wall for their meagre possessions, a few school materials and an item of clothing. There was only one bathroom, consisting of cold showers and a few holes in the ground.

The home was partly funded by a lady from the US and generous locals who provided food, books, clothing and money. The director of the home worked full-time with extended family members and a few underpaid staff. It was clear they survived week to week. I was compelled then and there to provide whatever support I could. I returned to Australia with a goal to raise the A$16,000 required to complete the building works and provide the space and facilities needed to support the growing home. I had never before sought to do something quite like this and didn't really know where to begin, but I was starting to find my way and a sense of purpose again.

6 Dark Days

I returned to Australia soon after, and Bec and I began organising our first major fundraising event. Our company put on a leadership seminar, secured speakers who volunteered their time, and we sold tickets within our network of clients. By the end of the day we had all experienced an inspiring seminar culminating with a networking event at our home. I went to bed that night feeling on top of the world, far from the dark days of earlier that year. Little did I know what was in store. The next day Bec and I realised we were facing the end of our marriage.

Bec and I married and had children at a young age. Neither of us truly understood the foundation required for a successful marriage, and were still finding our way in life. The truth was that we both had a suite of self-sabotaging behaviours, and couldn't understand why or how they came about. Mine involved an inability to communicate with Bec and share my feelings, and when under stress I would often retreat to my 'cave'. I would shut everyone out while I tried to work my way through difficult situations. I was often under a lot of pressure and by the time I had invested energy in my business, my clients and my kids there wasn't always much left for Bec. Bec's attempts to deal with these and her own family challenges tended to involve drinking a little too much, and when in this state she would seek the attention she wasn't getting from me. That night after one too many celebratory drinks, she made a decision that started a chain of events, causing enormous pain to both of us and bringing our marriage close to an end. In one day I had felt the elation of an enormously successful fundraising event and the despair of losing everything that was important to me.

I would like to say that there was a quick and easy transition to a better marriage and our new life, but it wasn't that easy. Bec and I spent several years rebuilding our relationship, learning to communicate, to listen and to fall in love again. We went to counselling, sold and moved to our little beach house on the coast, and reduced the hours we were working. We tried to draw life back to the most important elements of being a family. There was less of a focus on money and possessions, and more time spent talking and loving and caring for each other. We were living a simpler, healthier life. We developed a distance from the stresses in our life and slowly rebuilt our marriage.

I spent several years moving between the light and shade of life. Some days I struggled just to get out of bed, others I was energised by the new possibilities our new lifestyle was bringing. Our kids were happily settled in their new school and life was full of long beach walks and surfing. Our small coastal town was sublime. Bec and I were much closer than we ever believed possible. We had created a commitment to seeing life as more than just working to live. The events that led up to this, as difficult as they were, shocked us out of our comfort zones and out of autopilot. We found the courage to face up to our demons and learn more about ourselves; our shortcomings and our strengths. We created a vision of how we wanted our marriage and family to be and then set about achieving it. We finally found the courage to make the difficult decisions and always put our marriage and our kids first.

7 Travelling as a Family

In 2008 our third child Gus was born. Life was great, and while we had made many positive changes to our life, the fantasy of travelling together as a family with a spirit of adventure was one that we were yet to fulfil. I had shared with Bec my dream of taking extended leave and travelling around the world as a family but I just couldn't see how it could be achieved.

Once we had children we accepted the fact that we would not be able to travel again. India, however, was calling, and while I wanted to respond, I was not sure how it would be possible. My default position when I can't see a way forward is to become disappointed and frustrated and resolve that there is no possible solution. Bec, on the other hand, acts. She grabbed the laptop, did a quick online check, and before we knew it tickets were booked. We were on our way to India once more, this time with three kids in tow – the youngest only a few months old. We visited the now rebuilt children's home, and India, Maggie and Gus got to experience firsthand what it was like for the kids living there. It was beautiful to see them all playing together. Our confidence in travelling as a family was growing and our spirit of adventure was starting to take shape.

8 The Seed Begins to Grow

In September 2010 we were in Barwon Heads on holiday. The two life-changing questions had been rolling around in my head and mixing with our life experiences and dreams. In recent months I had watched Shane Crawford (a retired AFL footballer) run 900 kilometres from Adelaide to Melbourne for a fundraiser, and I had seen a documentary on Gandhi's walk across India. I had forgotten how to dream and was excited to suddenly feel inspired to do something similar.

The girls were still sleeping so Bec and I took Gus out of the camper. We walked down to the little playground in the park and as I pushed Gus on the swing Bec asked the inevitable question, 'So what's on your mind?' She could almost hear the cogs turning in my head and knew something was brewing.

'I want to walk across India.'

Bec was accustomed to my wild dreams and simply took a breath.

'Tell me more.'

The more we talked the more resolute I became about my goal. My only concern was how we could be together on such an epic journey. We did everything together and this would have to be the same.

Later that night in the Barwon Heads Pub we had a family meeting and asked the kids what they thought. Without taking breath, eleven-year-old Indy asserted, 'You're not going without me,' and my goal quickly became a family goal of walking together across India. We had no idea how we would go about it or even if we could do it, but immediately had a sense that it was something we would find a way to achieve. The one thing I knew about goal setting is that to move from a dream to a goal you have to tell people about it. So we did, starting with our family and friends. Each time we told someone the reality became a little clearer and the fear and awe of our goal began to emerge.

We knew that a project of this size required support and that we needed the help of those we trusted. So I went to two of my best friends – my mum Jenny and my stepfather Nick. Nick was immediately motivated by our goal, almost as though he was waiting for this family adventure to come along, and with little need of convincing, he and Mum were in. Nick and I have always been close. We were best men at each other's weddings and are more mates than father and son. Jen and Nick accompanied us previously to India and to East Timor and Thailand and are great travelling companions. Nick and Jen have a wonderful story. Mum was thirty, a single working mum with two kids when she met Nick – a fresh-faced nineteen-year-old. They immediately struck up a special bond and have kept it ever since. Nick worked his way through an accounting degree, followed up later in life with a law degree, all while working and supporting Mum to raise my sister and me. Throughout the years Nick never sought to be our father, but rather a mentor and friend, and is often referred to as the rock of our family because he always approaches things objectively and calmly. Mum is quite the opposite. She is always fighting for someone or something she believes has been hard done by and is highly emotional.

It is a rare phone call with Mum where she doesn't cry at some point. Mum's most important attribute though, for me at least, is that she has always loved my sister and me unconditionally. This has been one of the most critical lessons I have learned as a parent, as I have always known that no matter happens, Mum will be there for me.

My other best friend, my sister Kate, was also extended an invitation. Despite being a single mum struggling to get by financially, she could see that this was going to be an opportunity of a lifetime for her and her two kids Alice and Max. She would find a way to be involved. Kate is a larger-than-life character with a big crop of curly blonde locks and she loves getting involved in every activity, especially physical ones like kicking the footy. Kate is the one person in our family who will always make you laugh, often until your ribs hurt. Her tactics often include doing impressions of family members, as well as recalling the most detailed memories of life growing up. If you'd asked me as a young adult if there was any chance that Kate and I would do something like this together I would have nearly died laughing. Kate and I were anything but close when we started off in life, perhaps the symptom of growing up in a small house competing for attention and limited resources. It took us some years to build what is now a strong and special friendship. Bec and I met through Kate, as they studied nursing together and were good friends at uni. While it took a few years for each of us to find our place in our three-way friendship, we are now very close and the trip wouldn't be the same without Kate. So Kate, Ally and Max would meet us for an Indian Christmas in Bangalore and walk the final 400 kilometres to Chennai.

9 Preparing for our Trip

When we decided to walk across India we gave ourselves eighteen months to prepare – or perhaps to change our minds. Not only did we need to work out how we were going to walk across India with five kids, but we also set ourselves the difficult goal of raising A$30,000. We always self funded our travel so that every cent we raised went to our projects, so we had to ensure we had enough savings to pay for our trip. I also needed to make sure I could take eight weeks off work, which is no easy feat when you work for yourself and no work means no pay.

Our next major decision was where to direct the money from our fundraising. ChildFund is a very special organisation, one that we had donated funds to for children's projects in Kenya and Afghanistan, and the first one we thought of. I spoke with Di Mason and Rachel Murphy from their branch in Australia. They had great ideas and their experience and support was to prove invaluable. One of Di's ideas was to identify communities and children in need and for us to visit them on our walk across India. This way we could experience for ourselves the difference our funds were making. The focus for all of our projects has been simple; to improve the health, safety and education of children and the communities in which they live. The plan was starting to take shape.

Bec and I have very different ideas about planning. We have joked many times that Bec's thoughts go toward logistics, medical kits, maps, and every detailed item we could possibly want. I was thinking about walking across India dressed in a *lungi* (an Indian sheet that men wear like a short dress) with a staff in one hand. The reality was that we really didn't have any idea of what we were doing or what we were going to need. While Bec and I are both drawn to the romantic notion of adventure, neither of us is very equipped. I am not the handiest male you will ever meet. I had recently tried to fix one of the wardrobe doors in Gus's room that had come off the runners. About ninety minutes later, sweat dripping down my forehead, I finally gave up with at least one of the doors in pieces on the bedroom floor. Those carpenters on the DIY shows make it look so easy!

10 The Long Build-Up

The plan to allow eighteen months seemed like a good idea – it would give us plenty of time to prepare. What it also meant was plenty of time to second guess myself, lose confidence, or wonder if I was indeed crazy – as crazy as the looks people gave me when I told them of our plans. There was also enough time to question if I was selfishly involving my family in the quest. Every time I had a bad day or lost confidence in myself I lost confidence in my goal. Bec and I had always been impulsive adventurers. We would often make up our minds in the moment and then book our tickets before we could change our mind. In a matter of weeks we would be off. This was different. It was a long time between impulse and action and this often tested my resolve. Bec, on the other hand, knew how important this was to all of us, and if she was second-guessing herself you wouldn't have known. On the other hand, my doubt was settling in and developing from a moment of weakness to a dark cloud. I was beginning to lose confidence and looking for ways to pull out. Maybe we could just donate some money to ChildFund. People would understand, wouldn't they?

I had been spending time with Tim, a good mate of mine, who also had three young children and a beautiful wife. We immediately hit it off several years earlier when he started working with a client of mine, and we had a lot in common. We thought the same way about work, and enjoyed many long conversations about people and life – especially our family and how to make it all work. Tim was a fit guy but had been suffering from cancer. He bravely fought his way through to remission, but the cancer returned and he started chemotherapy again, which was difficult to watch. Tim was not the sort of guy who would make you worry about him; in fact he would often make a joke out of it. He was the youngest CEO in local government in Victoria – just to give you an insight to the calibre of his professional talents. On a personal level Tim was one of the funniest and most positive individuals I have ever had the pleasure of knowing. One day on a long drive we were talking about our families and how proud we were of our kids. Our walk intrigued Tim so much that he asked if he could join us for part of it. It was one of those small injections of motivation that I needed. If Tim thought it was a good idea then I couldn't be completely crazy.

I woke on what seemed like a normal July morning,

planning to work from home before heading out for meetings later that day. The phone rang. It was Paul, one of Tim's colleagues and also a good friend, who told me that Tim had passed away the day before. Everything stopped. I could function enough to respond to Paul, but my mind was in another place altogether. After the brief phone call, I sat by my desk and broke down. I cried like never before; a deep guttural cry that came from deep in my stomach. Bec came in to see me and we held each other in utter disbelief. How could this happen? I had been talking to Tim the week before about a project we were working on. As far as I was aware he had been making great progress. I later found out that this is what he wanted – for everyone to get on with their lives and not constantly be worrying about him and his treatment. How could I go to work that day? How could anybody? When a man of Tim's character and integrity passes away life should just stop.

Several days later we attended Tim's funeral with hundreds of others who felt just as we did. Tim was larger than life. He had a way of making you feel like you were the most important person to him. He was the same age as many of my friends and we all sat at his funeral thinking, Why Tim? This could have been any one of us. If I was having doubts before I was now pretty clear that the last thing I wanted to do was to put my life and the life of my family at risk. The walk was off. I made it through the funeral, the burial and the wake and headed to a local motel for the evening as I had agreed to help Tim's team work through their reactions to his passing. It seemed like a good offer at the time, but I was beginning to realise that there was no way I could help others when I couldn't even help myself. I remembered Tim raving about a local park and walking track. As I sat in my hotel room feeling shattered I felt the urge to do something, so I told myself to get off my arse and walk.

The park was beautiful. There was a path that meandered around two very large lakes with breathtaking flora and fauna. On this afternoon there were a few people walking and jogging but it was pretty quiet. Quiet enough for me to be lost in my thoughts and through the walk achieve a moment of clarity. Tim's passing was not a reminder to play it safe; it was a reminder that life is there to be lived. This was something I had to do to honour Tim's memory and, as Tim would be telling me, for my family and myself. When I got back to the room I rang Bec and with absolute conviction confirmed that the walk was not only back on, but it was now time to get serious.

11 Seven Weeks to Go

Walking across India was finally becoming a reality. Leading up to our departure date we had the inevitable 'oh crap' moments, but other than that we remained strong – or at least Bec did. She was the rock and she kept me looking ahead. We committed to raise the A$30,000 at least, speak at as many functions as we could, help the walk team get organised, and work in partnership with ChildFund. It was a daily activity for us. What were we thinking?

With seven weeks to go we had a draft route planned,

a few days of accommodation booked, our flights booked, our fundraising plans arranged, and had organised our shoes and our packs (with a great hit to our family budget). There was an equally long list of things yet to be completed. We did not have our final trip budget finalised, we hadn't confirmed our driver or support vehicle, much of our accommodation hadn't been booked, and our clothing hadn't been organised. I was slightly overweight and not quite in the physical condition I would've liked. My hips, knees and ankles were screaming out for a break and I just hoped all the joints would remain intact for the walk. Bec looked and felt great, Indy was super fit and training for a different sport everyday, and Maggie and Gus were opting in and out of physical preparations depending on their moods and what was on television. My walking partner, Nick, was regularly practising his long walks and had new shoes. Kate had lost twelve kilograms in preparation and both had their personal trainers whip them into condition, while Mum had a partial knee replacement.

Many of the challenges involved the preparation and planning – neither a strength of mine. To me, the walk was about a 'back to basics' trip to India: one bag, basic clothing, basic food and a journey for the soul. It's hard to explain but I feel that India, the country, is good for me spiritually. It reminds me of what's really important. Not the house, cars, or lifestyle we have back home, but the connection with people and the sense of genuinely being able to make a difference to others. It was the ability to be and feel a thousand miles away from the many trivial things that occupied my mind, time and efforts in the real world.

People often asked why I wasn't more diligent with planning what and where we would eat, where we would stay and how far we would get. I resisted because the adventure was about landing on the west coast of India, looking east, and starting to walk. I guess for a young, solo backpacker this would just be another overseas holiday, but when the trip involves five children and your parents, it becomes somewhat more of an adventure, and creates a very different dynamic. Multiple personalities, interests and opinions needed to be accounted for, and India would bring out the best and worst of everyone for all to see.

12 Our Major Fundraiser – Eighteen Days to Go

Our major fundraiser, a leadership seminar, took most of the year to plan and was a huge challenge for my confidence. There was that voice in my head that told me no one would come, and that I should cancel it to save face. Then when some people inevitably said no, didn't return my calls, or told me they were sorry but they weren't interested, that voice would laugh and say, 'I told you so.' Then when all seemed lost, someone would unexpectedly show support – an email from an old client, a good friend saying they wouldn't miss it – and little by little it all came together. The possibility of putting on an event for ninety people, with twelve talented guest speakers sharing their stories of inspiration, was an emotional prospect. Bringing people such as these together to make a difference in the lives of vulnerable kids was the reason for the walk, and the eventual support shown was incredible. It was the fuel we needed to complete our epic adventure.

One of the beautiful things about doing these events as a family is that your kids constantly keep you grounded. On the morning of the big day as we were busy finalising our talks and packing some last-minute items, Gus walked outside, took off his pants, and squatted in the middle of the driveway. Yep, anything can happen at anytime with Gus!

We eventually cleaned up Gus – and the driveway – and headed to the Frankston Arts Centre to put on our event. I dedicated the day to Tim. He was a skilled motivational speaker, obvious to anyone who met him. I couldn't think of a better way to honour my mate. I provided an update for the previous projects we had funded, including the children's home and school in Chennai, funding for a home for orphaned girls in Cambodia, and school projects in Kenya and Afghanistan.

Our keynote speaker for the day was Paul Hameister who climbed Mount Everest in May 2011. Paul was an inspiration and quite possibly the most disciplined and dedicated individual I have ever met. His planning and preparations put us to shame. Demonstrating absolute commitment, he explained in detail just what it took to be able to climb the seven summits culminating in his conquering of Mount Everest. He shared with the audience the danger involved and the narrow escapes he had leading up to his climb. He also told how he had been able to raise significant funds for a range of important initiatives including a children's home in Nepal.

There were many other inspirational speakers who had a personal story to share. Our day ended with a very special presentation for me and, as I later found out, the audience. Bec, together with our two amazing girls, inspired everyone as they shared the details of our commitment to raise awareness and funds for vulnerable children in India. I couldn't have been prouder of them; they spoke beautifully of their determination in making a difference in the lives of others.

I finished with a few words of thanks and recited some of Marianne Williamson's poem 'Our Greatest Fear', which reminded me of Tim. By the end of the day we had raised approximately A$35,000 for a range of critical projects for disadvantaged children in India, exceeding our fundraising goal. What an amazing sense of achievement and relief.

As I reflected on the day it reminded me how much people want to give when they are inspired and have an opportunity. I was so excited that we could achieve this on top of having a great day, honouring my friend, and raising considerable funds for our projects. I want to acknowledge everyone who gave support and inspired us to achieve our goals. Bec and I had a wonderful sense of calm resolve about our efforts and the challenges that lay ahead. We could now focus on our final preparations for the walk.

13 Two Days Until We Leave

It was Sunday night and for the first time in Petrucco family history we were actually packed the day before we left. It was a disciplined pack with only the absolute essentials included. The food bag and the medical kit were the biggest, because there was no way we wanted to run out of Vegemite or bandages! The kids had been very active in their sports and school activities and were spending time with their friends. We reluctantly sold our camper (to fund the overspend of the trip), travelled interstate, gave talks to different groups – including the media – made plans for our very old collie dog, planned to buy a new dog (ready for the kids when we got back), started a new business (ready for me when I got back), tried to fit in as many training walks as possible, and got ready to traverse India. Needless to say it was a big couple of weeks.

One morning Bec and Indy headed to Indy's school for a girls' morning tea. After *choplikarote*, an old Italian family favourite from my nonna, which was basically pancake mixture served like scrambled eggs, I decided to surprise Bec by cleaning out the camper for its new buyer. Gus decided golf on the back deck was far more interesting, but Maggie and her friend Tessa were very helpful for a while before getting tired and heading inside. They were back in a matter of minutes shouting that there was an emergency. Gus had taken great pleasure squirting the girls with the hose, but in the process had flooded the back of the house. Fortunately no real harm was done. Gus was into time-out to think about his efforts, the girls went back to practicing their dance routines, and I went back to the camper for more cleaning. But Gus wasn't finished yet. After time to regroup and consider his next assault, he grabbed the paint bottle and sprayed copious amounts everywhere. I was not impressed. The good news was that he hadn't made it to the new section of the deck. The bad news was that he had managed to get the back room of the house. Fortunately it was still in the process of being built, and the girls caught him just in time. I put Gus back into time-out and went back to my job. This time, after quiet contemplation, Gus informed me I had three strikes, that he was the one who wasn't impressed, and that I should be in time-out. You have to admire his bravado. I decided he was in need of some attention and the camper would have to wait.

One of the hardest parts of travelling with kids has to be the immunisations. Now whenever we discuss travel plans with our kids the first question is always, 'Do we need to get injections?' usually followed by, 'If we do I'm not coming!' For this trip, because we would be walking through rural areas, and were also likely to be around local wildlife and street dogs, we were having the full assault. Not only did this mean several thousands of dollars, but several needles over several weeks for the whole family. Maggie nearly fainted after one injection, and Gus had to be held down for his final rabies shot. You can only try and convince the kids so many times that it is for their health and safety.

14 Leaving Home

I may have claimed early credit for having completed our packing on time. Little did I know, we had only done a draft pack. Our plan was to drop the kids at school before packing the car, ready to get to the airport by lunchtime. I had an early appointment, Bec had a few errands to run, and we had just decided to arrange a couple of Christmas presents for the kids pillowcases (just in case Santa couldn't find us in Bangalore), before heading home to pack up.

Once home we remembered that we had to move furniture in Maggie's room before a wall could be knocked out while we were away, and clean out the home office. I took charge of this while Bec packed the final bag of food and medical supplies upstairs. When I went to check on her, she was sitting next to an over-packed suitcase, tears streaming down her face, claiming she was a little overwhelmed. For the woman who is widely known as the most positive individual on earth this was an unusual occurrence, but even she was beaten trying to fit an extra nine kilograms into the suitcase.

I suggested delaying our departure by a few hours, and Bec quickly recovered after a big hug and a couple of deep breaths. We picked up the kids from school, said our goodbyes to Molly, our collie, and headed to the airport. Bec continued her emotional day saying goodbye to our home on the Mornington Peninsula, a part of the world she had fallen in love with. She and I sat in the front catching up on phone messages and emails, distracted by the reprisal of 'Sexy and I Know It' sung by Maggie and Gus. Indy stared out the window pining for Molly. They had been together almost since birth so it was difficult for her to say goodbye. Molly was thirteen years old, with grey hair all over, only a handful of teeth left, and a very old set of bones. It was always going to be touch and go whether she would still be with us when we left on the trip. We just hoped she could hold on until we got home. We had decided to get her a roommate; a black labrador named Jasper who we had arranged to pick up on return from India. 'Wiggle wiggle wiggle, yeah' came streaming from the back seat, as Gus merrily held his own against his big sister.

We had a good run to the airport and arrived on time to drop off our car at the long-term parking lot. By this time Gus had of course fallen asleep, only to awake a little more grumpy and definitely not in the mood for singing. Bec and Indy went in to sort out the car booking while I started to unload the four backpacks, the medical and food cases and the two remaining kids. Indy came running back moments later and told me to reload the car, as the company we had planned to leave our car with for the six weeks had gone out of business only forty-five minutes earlier. Great timing. Fortunately there was a competitor just down the road. Take two was more successful, and we loaded the gear and kids into the minibus and headed off to the hotel for our last night in Australia.

Jen and Nick met us at the hotel, which the kids were very excited about. Gus and Maggie played trampolines on the bed and the peaceful serenity of the hotel room lasted all of about fifteen seconds. Bec packed and repacked her bags and the kids bags, and we pushed the two double beds together to make one massive family bed for the five of us to sleep in, with Jen and Nick just down the hall. We said goodnight, dreamed a little more about the adventures that lay ahead, and prepared ourselves for Master Gus and an eleven-hour flight to Kochi via Singapore.

PART TWO

India

Day 1
The Long, Long Journey to India

We all slept well and awoke to the view of planes flying in and out of Melbourne Airport. I asked Bec if she had managed to transfer funds into our account for us to access while we are away, to which she confidently replied it had all been taken care of. Minutes later, however, I noticed her tapping away on her phone on our online account. We shared a laugh. I am very good at pointing out, in hindsight, all the things we should have done – one of those annoying traits where I manage to ask just the right question at the wrong time. This was the first of many such questions, but luckily Bec and I have developed an understanding and now it plays out as friendly banter.

We repacked our backpacks, medical case and supplies case, loaded up to the hilt and walked down to check out. By the time we'd made it down the few floors to the lobby Maggie expressed her distaste at carrying her new backpack, although she did like the whole 'Aussie backpacker' look. We checked in, checked our bags onto the flight, and were on our uneventful way.

Bec danced along the path in the airport much to Maggie's disgust, who quickly separated herself from what she declared to be an embarrassing sight. We had a rest stop at Cafe Vue for coffee and croissants. Bec took snaps on her camera, but whenever someone tried to take Gus's photo, he responded with his new line – 'no paparazzi'. He soon discovered it would be a regular occurrence. Nick, after receiving directions from Gus, ordered him a purple macaroon. As it turned out was beetroot flavoured – not that Gus seemed to mind. He had dressed himself that morning so of course his pants were on back-to-front, although he did manage to get his shoes on the right feet. He sat at the table blowing bubbles in his OJ, looking quite the intrepid traveller.

On our way through security we had our next problem of the trip with the realisation that Indy had left her iPad behind. It was mainly for entertaining Gus, so Bec was far from thrilled. Nick turned a lighter shade of white as he sheepishly declared that he had left his new laptop in his checked baggage, which sent him into a bit of a self-loathing meltdown. The text we received from our house-sitter saying that Grandma Molly had woken this morning in good spirits worked well to distract us and made us all a little happier.

As we went to leave I realised Bec had left her camera at the cafe and had to rush back to grab it. Fortunately it was still there. I wondered to myself whether it would be worth taking bets from the walk team to see how long it would be before Bec would lose her new camera. As we sat and waited to board I thought about the diversity of people you find at airports heading in different directions for different reasons. I would love to interview people about their onward journeys just to share in their upcoming experiences. Indy seemed to share no interest in this, and commented that she didn't like the smell of airports; reminiscing about her very dark days flying into LAX when she became very ill. We had about five days of Indy vomiting every twenty minutes, and were all severely jetlagged in a hotel undergoing major renovations. There is probably nothing worse than being overseas, a long way from home and in a place where you know nothing and no one. We spent several days in and out of local hospitals and emergency centres as we tried to get treatment. Having no luck, we moved to a nicer hotel and arranged for the hotel driver to take us to yet another clinic. This time we ended up in a backyard of someone's house, which we quickly determined wasn't going to cut it. Exhausted and quickly running out of ideas, we decided to get out of Los Angeles and head for Santa Monica. We fortunately found a paediatric hospital that was like a mirage. Indy was put straight into a clean hospital bed, onto a drip and took a barrage of tests. Those of you with kids would probably relate to how quickly Indy then moved from what appeared to be near death to eating hot dogs. Even in the US where you expect everything to be fine, this served as a timely reminder of the challenges of travelling with kids.

Indy was now writing in her journal and reading comments from the many different adventures she had already been on. This gave her an immediate sense of perspective and she commented on how great it was to be doing something to help kids we met on previous trips. Maggie, on the other hand, was sitting on Nick's lap checking his brain (a Maggie thing she did with her Poppa) and commented she believed it was the size of a pea. Bec was slowly unwinding. It had been such an incredible build-up, and those past few hours had been a bit of a roller-coaster. I could feel Bec slowly starting to get her equilibrium back and relax. I had Gus in my arms, and he took full advantage of the situation as he started poking me in the eye, licking up and down my cheeks, and putting my glasses on and off my face. He is never one to miss an opportunity.

We made it to gate nine on time to board our flight SQ238 on the new Airbus A380. We found our seats just as the engines started to hum, a child cried further up the plane, and the captain over the intercom informed us of a small technical issue that would keep us waiting for a few more minutes. Gus decided it was time to stretch out across three seats – his head on my lap and feet on Bec. Indy sat on the other side next to me, while Maggie sat with Jen and Nick. I glanced over and noted that Indy had written 'calm' on the back of her hand – something I think she picked up from school to help her focus. Like me, she is a born worrier, and when there is a lot happening she can get herself quite worked up.

Maggie and Gus took off their shoes and a slight odour wafted its way through rows forty-two and beyond. Bec reminded me quietly that this could be the opportunity for me to write my book – something I had dreamed about for years. I often relate to the character out of the movie *Mr Holland's Opus* in which Mr Holland, a musician, dreams to write an opus, but is constantly distracted by the demands of life and family and it is not until his retirement that his life's work comes together. Could this be my journey too? In the back of my mind I had another private BHAG goal to write and inspire others to follow their dreams, which I was embarrassed about and certainly fearful of, but I believe that if you don't tell others about your ambitions they will never come to pass.

As the plane began to move down the runway I had regular yet fleeting thoughts about what lay ahead of us. I wondered if this was like the movie *The Perfect Storm* when they sit in calm waters making the decision to push on through the approaching storm. I shared my thoughts with Bec and she gave me a reassuring smile. There were the obvious fears about the kids' safety, my own physical conditioning or lack of, the logistics of the trip, and the many challenges that lay ahead. My immediate fear was not knowing which direction to go on day one of our walk. It seemed like it might be a good idea to buy a map just in case. The cabin crew were making final preparations; seatbelts on, window shades up. Bec was tossing up between the beef curry and pan-fried chicken for lunch, and Indy was starting to relax a little more and was staying calm. The hand tattoo must have been working. Gus yelled out to Maggie, 'The Man says we have to turn our tellies off. Maggie. Maggie. MAGGIE!' Gus's voice was muffled by his nungi – his dummy. He also had two in his left hand and one in his right just in case – he was well stocked for the trip. I looked around and noticed the Christmas wreaths adorning the cabin of the plane as Bec leant over to whisper that she had dreamed of this moment for so long. 'It's really happening,' she said to me and off we went – our adventure of a lifetime. Thoughts of work, friends, family and Molly slowly moved out of my mind, the wheels folded up into the wings, as Gus asked, 'What's that?' 'Just the plane noises,' Bec calmly advised. He snuggled in for a cuddle and I held him just a little tighter.

I took a moment to look at my family and thought to

myself, 'How did I get this lucky?' Bec is my world, and the most beautiful and inspiring woman I know. Together we have experienced the darkest depths and the highest and brightest highs – certainly more than I would have ever dreamed or feared – and we continue on, stronger for all the experiences we have shared. Gussy fell asleep, nungis in hands and mouth, and awoke two hours later with blond dreadlocks going in all directions, very excited about the lunch tray that awaited him. Unfortunately he slept a little too well, and being a morning sleep he didn't have his night-time nappy on. Accidents happen.

Indy reached over to whisper in my ear that she was excited about being in India again. It was lovely to see her confidence growing. She took a dose of Phenergan, with Maggie following suit, and both were gently sedated for the flight. Flying economy class internationally (the only way we travel) is not very glamorous, and being stuck in a small space with young children for many hours is a recipe for disaster. We were thankful that our kids travel well.

As we came in to land Gus started coughing and dry retching. Bec dived for the chuck bag, but didn't have the dexterity to open it in time. I stayed poised, hands cupped in front of Gus, ready to do what I had to. Fortunately it was a false alarm. By the time Bec got the bag open it was required. Nothing unusual for us; in fact it was a welcome relief only needing one bag for the trip.

We had a six-hour wait in Singapore before our flight to Kochi. We walked into Changi Airport with Nick still stewing about his laptop and deciding he was determined to retrieve it before the next flight. As we gathered ourselves in the waiting area, Mum noticed that Bec had left her camera behind. Bec and Maggie ran back to retrieve it as Gus ran the gauntlet up and down the travelator. Good news; the camera was located and Bec learnt her lesson – she didn't take it off her neck for the rest of the trip.

We made the pilgrimage to the orchid garden in Changi and Gus fell in love with the big fish in the pond, spending much of the six hours running around the ponds playing with them. Aside from the occasional photo with the stray tourist who would ask if they could get a photo with Gus, shortly followed by a quick touch of his long blond hair, Bec was quickly relaxing back to the old Buddha Mama we know and love. A couple of hours later and Nick managed to get his laptop back in one piece, although unfortunately in the process, Mum realised she left her prescription sunglasses behind, which resulted in a brief lowering of morale.

Six hours passed relatively quickly, and we headed to the gate to board our next flight. It sunk in that we were travelling to India, as we fast became a minority at the boarding gate. We were also no longer on the A380, but downsized to a very small and very old A319. We had unfortunately been seated in rows twenty-three and twenty-four – one from the rear of the plane. At the check-in lounge I rapidly filled in immigration forms for the five of us, which effectively at 1 am Melbourne time was not the easiest or most enjoyable of tasks. It was also in the 'meltdown zone' for Gus, and it was always touch and go as to whether he would fall asleep or have a hyperactive meltdown. Fortunately this time he fell asleep on Indy and me, and he and Maggie slept for most of the flight. I, on the other hand, was cooped up trying to keep Gus still and asleep, and poor Indy was constantly awoken by a combination of Gus stirring, cabin lights shining directly on her, and general discomfort. Jen and Nick were tucking into their chicken curry and making full use of the rediscovered laptop as I just tried to get through the flight and keep Gussy asleep – we did not want him to wake up a couple of hours out of Kochi. It turned out to be a very long four hours on an uncomfortable flight with bad turbulence. As we were preparing for our descent, Gus sat bolt upright telling us, and anyone who cared to listen, about the 'Walking With Dinosaurs' show we went to recently. He regaled the back rows of the plane with stories of *T. rexs* and long necks and an excited surprise that his (imaginary) friend Slime had joined in for our expedition.

We landed in India in the middle of the night very tired. It was an immediate reality check, prompting the question, 'Are we crazy?' We made our way to the immigration counter among an impatient crowd, jostling for position. Fortunately for all, our plane was the only late arrival and there were plenty of counters available. The seated Indian gentleman who served us passed a cursory look our way, and we replied with the customary Aussie 'G'day mate', which seemed to have little impact on our new friend. He conscientiously worked his way through each passport and immigration form, asking for each member of the team one at a time and checking that they were who we said they were. Gus had a passport photo from when he was three months old, so I wasn't exactly sure how they made the connection to the three-year-old that now stood before them. Perhaps the crankiness was enough to motivate him to stamp the passport and move us along.

After what seemed like an eternity we proceeded to the baggage counter and waited nervously to see if there were any further surprises. Despite our commitment to travel light, between the seven of us there were still several trolleys loaded up to the hilt. Unlike the usual frantic experience arriving at Melbourne Airport, the baggage collection process at Kochi was remarkably calm and ordered.

The car to the hotel was waiting for us as we left the airport – we felt blessed for small mercies and introduced ourselves to our driver Gus, pronounced 'Gooz'. Many families were reunited, and happy faces surrounded us as they headed off into the dark night with their suitcases and bundles. The air was comfortably warm, and we were tired but excited that our journey had finally begun. We were in India at last.

It was now the very early hours of the morning and the usual incredible Indian hustle and bustle was replaced with a very quiet and surreal experience – aided by the wonder of seeing our first elephant wandering past on the highway. Given the speed we were travelling, I guessed our driver was keen to get back to the hotel, and although I was tired I watched carefully for any incident he might have missed in his haste. Indian traffic has a nasty habit of surprising you when you least expect it. We made it to the hotel and quickly checked into our rooms. There were five of us in a one-bedroom room, and although we had ordered a couple of trundle beds, the customary Indian way is to await arrival, and then provide the bed in the guests' presence. The two young men from housekeeping took great pride in making the bed and it was fast becoming clear that our small room would not cater for any more than one extra bed. Indy quickly secured rights to it, and Maggie and Gus made themselves comfortable with Bec and me. We were too tired to notice the crowded sleeping arrangements, and quickly fell into a deep sleep. As I drifted off I saw images of crowded airports, the empty streets, and the elephant strolling nonchalantly down the road.

Day 2 Rest Day in Kochi

We awoke at 6.30 am, with everyone feeling better for a good nights sleep, to a strikingly beautiful Indian sunrise. I could see why the sign welcoming us to Kerala referred to it proudly as 'Gods Own Country'. Our colonial-style hotel was built right on the water's edge. Although we were on the fifth floor, it was almost as though we were at water level and looking out the window of a ship. As we sat and drank our morning tea, we could see boats gliding past over long lengths of weed, and a guard sitting on a chair many floors below our room, half asleep and cuddling a very old rifle. Gus, now fully recharged, was requesting lollies for breakfast – he had caught a glimpse of them in the food case the night before and was very excited about the prospect of an in-room meal. It was Nick's birthday and he got plenty of attention from the kids who were happy to share his special day. Feeling very physically tired after the many hours travelling the day before, I struggled to do a couple of early morning stretches, trying desperately to build up some core strength – without great success I might add. Fair to say after more than fifteen hours of international travel my body was not in good shape.

We got dressed quickly, very hungry for breakfast, and headed down to the buffet – the kids favourite Indian activity. It was well stocked with every imaginable breakfast item. There were many staff – all male – who were eager to provide service. In contrast to the airport, the hotel was predominantly stocked with westerners; Americans and Europeans judging from the snippets of conversation I could hear. We offered friendly good mornings, but most guests didn't return smiles with the same level of enthusiasm. Perhaps they weren't too excited to have three noisy kids impose on their peaceful breakfast plans. Not to be deterred, the Petrucco kids made themselves at home.

I enjoyed a predominantly traditional Indian breakfast, which consisted of curry, samosas, fresh fruit, and five cups of south Indian coffee. It was our favourite, sweet beverage that we assumed was made with condensed milk, and quickly grew on Indy and Mags.

After a very hearty breakfast we took a walk around the gardens and along the water's edge. Large ocean liners and ships full of containers cruised by only a stones throw from our hotel. The pool was looking very cloudy much to the disappointment of the kids, and we determined they should leave swimming for today – just in case. Gus already had developed a plane cough and a day in the pool was not likely to help. He did, however, find a trike in the gardens and spent some time cruising around the hotel grounds on his newly acquired three-wheeler. The crows were arguing, while small Indian squirrels scurried up and down trees. There were ibises sitting on the reeds, and coconut trees and frangipanis aligning the hotel's garden. The air was warm, and as I followed Gus speeding around on his trike, Christmas carols faintly streamed from the hotel, interspersed with Indian pipe music blaring out of several boats cruising by. It was all somewhat surreal. There was a light haze over the large expanse of water that marked the entry into Kochi Harbour. Across the channel thousands of containers were visible in the shipyard waiting to be dispersed to their next location. The warmth of the sun slowly increased – it was going to be a hot day.

As I looked up at the balcony above the pool, an older businessman sat in a comfortable-looking chair, while his servant stood close behind. They stayed in that position for some time – the sight of the awaiting servant was unusual for us. A barge chugged by as two young blond boys ran by the water; a woman with a baby in her arms was in hot pursuit. Fish and turtles could be seen swimming nearby. Maggie was sitting in front of me practising drinking out of a bottle Indian style, with a frangipani tucked behind her ear. She needed some practice drinking from the bottle without it touching her lips, and it kept us all amused for some time. Of course Indy started losing patience with her inexperienced little sister, and took over to show her how it was done.

Jen suggested that we should catch a ferry across to the mainland to see if we could stock up on some supplies. Many things on our list were yet to be acquired. We decided to meet down in the lobby in twenty minutes to head off. We walked to our room to experience the first run of living out of our packs.

Well, we had hair problems, shoe problems, shorts problems, sunscreen problems and a few heated discussions between the kids about which item belonged to which person. It was a slightly hostile mix of tiredness, jetlag and disorganisation. All of this disarray meant that despite only being a ten-minute walk from the ferry, and running the last stretch, we did not get there in time to board. The next one was not for another hour. Bec and I took the opportunity to head back to the hotel with Indy in tow and put our money in the safe, which we had neglected to do. On the way a large rally was forming for a group who referred to themselves as the CPEO. There were many red flags and several people giving speeches. One thing I have always tried to steer clear of when travelling in foreign countries is public demonstrations, and I shared this with Bec and Indy. My point hit home as a loud bang erupted nearby. We put our heads down and kept walking – a little faster this time. No one at the rally seemed particularly concerned, and I couldn't see anyone or anything that looked like a threat. Bec turned white, and Indy looked a little worried, but if she was she didn't share it with us at the time.

Gus and the girls loved the short ride across to the mainland. The ferry was a small boat fitted out internally with many rows of pews running parallel throughout the interior. It was quite busy, with Indian people of all ages. The kids were getting a lot of attention – something else they needed to get used to as they did stand out in the crowd. Bec and the kids took a seat and I stood up, enjoying the slightly cooler air coming off the water into the open windows of the boat. As we arrived at the mainland, the boat pulled up alongside several others that were tied to the jetty. The route to go ashore was to walk through our boat, and then through two others before making our way to the jetty. It was one of those moments where you think to yourself, Only in India. We followed the crowd and it all just seemed to be part of the way things were done around here. The street was adorned with market stalls and we were once again in the hustle and bustle of Indian life on the streets. People were everywhere, with every type of transport buzzing by in every direction. I grabbed Gus and put him on my shoulders, and we reminded the girls to stay close and keep their wits about them.

We soon became stuck as we carefully attempted to cross a particularly busy street on our quest to find Mahatma Gandhi (M.G.) Road. There we were, all seven of us, standing on the side of the road waiting patiently to cross. The traffic was moving very quickly, ranging in size from bicycles to buses, and no sizeable break presented itself. Our cautious approach was not going to get us anywhere, so we aligned ourselves with a couple of locals – an adult next to every child – took a deep breath, and walked out into the traffic. No pedestrian crossings here, and if we hadn't gone then we might still be waiting.

By then it was getting hotter and busier, and walking was uncomfortable. We decided to prioritise our list, focusing on internal communications and foregoing the hunt for a number of other items. We managed to get some money changed, and then located a series of mobile phone stores where Nick bought Indian SIM cards for his old Australian mobiles – only once he had supplied copies of his passport, however. The girls were getting tired and thirsty, and we enjoyed taking a minute off the streets and cooling down in front of some fans.

We flagged down a couple of autos for the ride back to the ferry. These were basically small carriages on a motorised trike that sounded like they ran on dried apricots. The kids loved the experience and we were back on the ferry in no time – a pretty good investment for a couple of dollars. Day one in India was drawing to a close, and after our somewhat brief interaction with the Indian traffic we were becoming well aware that we had a very challenging experience in front of us.

The jet lag kicked in and most of us were ready for bed by 7 pm. The hotel sent up a bedtime story for Gus, but fortunately he had already fallen asleep on my lap. Maggie was determined to get a 'Barry Evil' story out of Nick, much to Jen's concern. Nick's stories were legendary among the kids in our family. He had a wonderful way of drawing from his childhood experience and created a wide range of mythical characters. Mum knew that the stories were all-consuming and often whipped the kids up into a frenzy – not to mention that they took Nick out of the adult conversation for some time. Nevertheless, Nick shared a short story with the kids – mainly to placate Maggie who was insistent that she deserved a story after the trip she endured to get there. We then had a planning meeting about the coming days, and it was an early night for all.

Day 3 Kochi to Kozhikode

Gus awoke at 3 am with his 'travellers cough', which resulted in lights on for everyone. Fortunately he was back to sleep half an hour later. We all awoke again at 6.30 am – almost like clockwork. Maggie and Gus decided to play 'Wiggle, wiggle, wiggle, yeah' on my bottom. They thought it was funny, but to me it was a reminder that I was not yet in walking shape.

A cruise ship went by and sounded a loud horn. Gus let out an, 'Oh shit!' Indy asked if he meant, 'Oh ship!'

'No,' Gus replied. Maggie suggested Gus should say, 'Oh shivers,' or, 'Jeepers creepers.'

'No. I say shit.'

He must get that from his mum.

There was another beautiful sunrise as we dressed for breakfast. Ibis, eagles and crows flew in front of our window, with the ibis finding their feet and landing on the reeds floating in the water. Meanwhile, Gus had advanced from swearing to pretending to be a doctor, using my pen as a needle. He went to great lengths to explain to me it wouldn't hurt because it was a small needle – something we used to help him through his immunisations. Bec was on tea duty, but she took a moment to give Gus a plastic syringe to his great delight.

Fashion-conscious Maggie was getting dressed, and Bec and I were providing suggestions about what we believed would be culturally appropriate. Unfortunately her favourite short shorts and off-shoulder T-shirts didn't make the cut. 'Oh my god, Dad,' was soon followed by a more detailed complaint to Bec: 'Dad wants to dress me in a snowsuit.' This was followed by a lecture from me on culture and appropriateness of dress; Maggie zoned out. It was a conversation we would have many times. She turned to her sister for help. Everyone was looking great in their Coast to Coast T-shirts made for the trip. Indy and Maggie earned an eight out of ten for effort and speed. Gus scraped through with a six.

I took advantage of the internet access and made sure I had the first leg of our route from Calicut to Kunnamangalam planned in detail. I was having this recurring nightmare that we started our walk with fifty people following us, and didn't know where to go. I made an impromptu map on a piece of paper, and our route for day one at least was planned.

We packed our bags and headed down to the lobby to check out. The hotel provided a warm send off with twenty staff giving the kids gifts, food and water for the trip. It was incredible hospitality to welcome us on our first few days in India. The Tempo Traveller – our transport for the next six weeks – arrived. It was a cross between a troop carrier and a 1980s panel van, very flash and well beyond our expectations with good air conditioning and comfortable seats. Our friendly and safety-conscious driver Raju helped us put on the kid's seatbelts. The kids related well to this young Indian man with long fingernails and blond streaks in his dark hair. In Indian culture long fingernails are a symbol of wealth. As trendy Raju grabbed the gearstick I noticed his four-centimetre-long thumbnail.

I could not do justice to the sights, sounds and smells of just a hundred metres of traffic in India. There were people bustling around the shops and colourful houses, which were surrounded by tropical trees and vegetation. There was rubbish everywhere, but it only partly spoiled the beauty of the Indian countryside. We drove past an elephant on the back of a van only slightly larger than it – another sight where you rub your eyes to make sure you aren't dreaming. I glanced out of the window to see a small silhouette of a man at the top of very tall powerlines, with no safety ropes to speak of. He at least had a plastic helmet, but it seemed to be more for show than effect. Everywhere you looked there was the mixture of old and new.

The girls were very excited about our new bus, and decided to christen it with their rendition of 'Eye of the Tiger', followed by the entirety of 'Ninety-Nine Bottles on the Wall'. We were all glad when that was over. Gus spent a while taking in the scenery, but quickly decided he had had enough and fell asleep for several hours. The first thing he said as he woke up was, 'Dammit. I forgot to raise my money for goats!' Everyone taking part in the walk was raising funds for a project. We assured Gus that he had done this, and the goats would be bought and shared with some of the families we would encounter. I think he was expecting we would have the goats in the van with us.

Unfortunately after five hours into the seven-hour journey, the vehicle was getting a bit much for Gus, who was still battling his cough. After a particularly bad coughing fit we decided to stop to avoid any follow through. As luck would have it we stopped in front of a school, and kids came from everywhere to say hello. Bec got her camera out for a shot, but each time she lifted it the children dropped down behind a wall. Then they would pop up again. This dance continued for a while before they gave in and Bec got her photo.

We got back in the car and finished our journey to the old Kappad Beach Hotel, which was a forty-five minute drive from the closest town through a labyrinth of small roads and backstreets. We made this booking online, which is always a bit risky. The hotel was undergoing renovations, and there were very few people around as we wandered through the grassed grounds toward our rooms. The hotel was situated only metres from the sand, with an old pool that looked unsafe for swimming, and surrounded by coconut trees. The rooms were very basic but comfortable, and the concrete balcony had a swinging egg chair that overlooked the ocean. Although it was getting late in the day as we headed out to the beach for a short walk, the sun was still very hot. The girls had a packet of chips and a Pepsi, while the rest of us enjoyed cups of Indian tea from one of the small tea stalls adjoining the beach. The stall was constructed from three pieces of galvanised iron tied together, a small fire and a saucepan for tea and coffee. The tea tasted like a milky, sweet chai – something we remembered well from previous visits.

After a short rest in our rooms we headed down for dinner. It turned out that aside from us, there was only one other couple staying in the hotel. As the hotel's renovations included the restaurant, we ate outside on a circular stage some twenty metres wide, overlooking the beach under a near-full moon. Despite still being quite tired, the ceremony of the occasion was not lost on us. The girls started up a game of scopa, which was an Italian card game I used to play growing up that was now a family tradition. Bec and I took turns following Gus as he tracked bugs and lizards in the copious gardens surrounding our dining stage until one of the waiters sensed the need for support and took over. Dinner was a beautiful selection of vegetarian curries, such as aloo gobi and palak paneer, and Indian breads. The girls did little to leave their comfort zone and tried the spaghetti Napoletana. Gus just wandered around. Before the end of the meal, he popped up with a baby lizard in hand, put it on the stage, and bedazzled it with a bright torch. Very proud, the budding Steve Irwin surveyed his captive until we could convince him to let it return home. We went off to bed that night relaxed about the journey so far. We had experienced moments of beauty and serenity, and utter madness and despair, and it was only our third day.

Day 4 The Walk Begins: Kappad Beach – Calicut – Kunnamangalam

It was 5.30 am and I was sitting alone on the balcony of our hotel room, taking one of those rare moments for quiet contemplation. For so long the trip had been about planning, but now it was really happening. It was hard to imagine what the following days would have in store for us. Would it be everything we hoped for or would it be a diabolical failure? Thankfully, as a family, we understood that we would have to be prepared for a combination of the two. At that stage I was just happy we had made it that far and that the walk was going to begin.

The crows were making a ruckus in the distance, the waves gently rolled onto the shoreline, and occasionally someone would along the path between our room and the beach. Maggie soon joined me on the balcony; a little weary-eyed but happy. She complained that she couldn't sleep because her mattress was too hard. She clambered into the cane egg chair and we started to think of names for our car to welcome it into the family.

Mum called out from her balcony in the adjoining room, happy to finally have company after being up for hours. Maggie, seeing I was writing, asked to add to our book, so I played typist as she dictated a few thoughts on the trip so far: 'It was so fun yesterday when Gus peed in the bottle on the bus. At about 8 pm last night, little Master Gus was hunting for animals and luckily one of the staff looked after him while we enjoyed our many spices of our dinner.'

She commented that she was still unsure about the name for our bus. Maggie often drifts from subject to subject, so it pays to try and keep up. She continued: 'Was it yesterday? No, it wasn't yesterday. The day before yesterday we went to town and it was very busy and there were so many people crossing the road and almost getting hit by tuk-tuks, taxis and trucks. Yesterday when we got out of the car we met a lovely little school with lots of little girls and boys who were very interested in the white-skin family that stopped for a clean up.'

Meanwhile, Gus had joined us, informing everyone that he had the best dream about possums, dinosaurs and squirrels. Bec followed Gus with the mosquito repellent, and Indy strolled out to sit next to me in the cane chair. Bec pointed out a little fishing boat chugging by.

Back to Maggie.

'Mum tried to take a photo and everyone hid like a game of hide-and-seek. Poppa took a video so he could film the little heads bobbing up and down behind the brick wall. Last night I almost broke my toe. Blood was squirting everywhere, as Nurse Ratchet tried to fix me with Betadine. She didn't stop after I said to and just ended up hurting me more.'

Nurse Ratchet was the affectionate nickname we created for Bec after she once rubbed Dencorub into an open rash on my leg. Although basic first aid is not her strong suit, she is actually a talented critical care nurse, who you would want close by in a real emergency.

Indy suggested that Maggie had just scraped a little bit of skin off her toe, and an argument unfolded. Maggie quickly got distracted and continued her story.

'Well yesterday when we went to the beach I wore my short shorts, and all the Indian men and women were staring at me like I was a massive freak with a massive egg hanging out of my head.'

'I told you to wear something else,' Indy informed her, smugly. Maggie ignored the quip from her big sister, and finished off by telling her friends in class 3B that she was having fun, but not too much.

Meanwhile a fishing boat drifted by, casting nets as the men slapped the water to get the attention of the fish. The rest of the family headed across to see Mum and Nick, and my serenity was momentarily restored. The sun was slowly rising, and it was once again possible to see the beauty of the Indian coastline. I couldn't enjoy it for long, however, as I had to check my notes to make sure I had the right directions to get us from Colicut, where we would commence our walk, through to Kunnamangalam. We planned to walk along Mavoor Road through to the medical college, and past the Indian Institute of Management on our way to Kunnamangalam. Raju would then pick us up and return us to the hotel. I hoped we wouldn't get lost, not on our first day.

We headed down for the walker's breakfast of omelettes and French toast, washed down with South Indian coffee. Soon enough we were into the car with Raju, and off to our departure ceremony at the Gateway Hotel in Colicut. As we left we crossed a bridge and, watching a fisherman in his small wooden boat shovelling out water due to a leak, I thought about the simplicity of life. We were a long way from the usual trials and tribulations of suburbia.

We passed a butcher with a goat hanging in the window, never a pleasant site, and many fish stalls by the side of the road as we ran the gauntlet of Indian traffic. There were school kids and adults everywhere. The kids sat up front and sang the Boom de Yada song from some Discovery Channel ads – which they learned on their last trip to India – and Christmas carols. The nervous excitement of the team made it seem like the morning of a big game. Everyone looked great in their green ChildFund T-shirts, and Bec and Nick decided on plaits and a bandana respectively for their signature looks. Nick was riffling through his backpack, and Mum informed him he was like an old lady with a handbag, never able to find what he was looking for.

Unfortunately we got lost en route, and seemed to drive around in circles for hours in our hunt for the hotel. As we drove along the esplanade, I admired the sets of very clean waves coming in and crashing on the shore. Out of desperation, Raju started asking for directions, and for the next thirty minutes we went up and down what felt like the same streets, with lots of discussions and head wobbling as we tried to secure directions to our destination. Just when all hope seemed lost, we arrived out of nowhere at the Gateway Hotel.

We all jumped out of the bus to a rock-star welcome. Our good friends from ChildFund – Dola, Antony, and Naomi – greeted us with many hugs and kisses, while a crowd of ChildFund staff, volunteers, and sponsored children were waiting in several rows of chairs. There were television cameras and reporters everywhere, which was completely unexpected and overwhelming. I had assumed we would be met by just a handful of ChildFund people who would join us for the walk on that first day. I momentarily recalled telling the walk team that we would quietly walk across India and no one would even know we were there. In true Indian tradition there was a stage set up, and we listened to a series of inspiring speeches from the staff. I was asked to speak, but was outshone by the kids and Bec who are never short of a word.

At this point there were camera crews surrounding us, and every member of our team was doing an interview. Gus was carried off and photographed with different people; his long blond locks were a major attraction, and an usual sight I was sure. I could sense that he had met enough people for one day so I rescued him and kept hold of him to calm him down. For a boy who was used to a lot of attention, even this was over the top. India and Maggie had both given interviews with the press, and Mum and Nick were enjoying discussions with many of the people who were joining us in the walk for the first day. Bec took the opportunity to have a quick meeting with Naomi from ChildFund, who had kindly offered to help us find accommodation along the way.

It was getting hot and a little late in the morning, so we decided to start the flag-off ceremony. Everyone from ChildFund – around sixty people in total – were lined up behind three large 'Coast to Coast' banners. Photographers would be walking ahead of us, like we were Brad and Angelina! Gus, getting a bit fed up with the whole situation, retreated to my shoulders where he would stay for the next three kilometres as we walked to our first rest stop, the Baby Memorial Hospital. As we walked through the streets, the crowd started chanting, 'We are ChildFund. We are for the children', and we managed to attract a great deal of interest. It was a surreal experience. Walking the streets in India is crazy enough, but we were in a crowd of people who rushed into the maddening traffic and stopped the cars to allow us to cross very busy roads.

The kids and I walked ahead, while Mum, Bec and Nick were in a group behind. We had been walking for a short time when Maggie piped up to inform me that Jen had fallen on the cobbled Indian roads. Bec swung into Nurse Ratchet mode and dived into her medical kit. Mum was, as you can imagine, a little disappointed and embarrassed by the attention. She was very brave given she had a partial knee replacement only weeks before, and despite the obvious damage, she was not to be stopped from completing that section of the walk.

We made it to the first stop without any more problems, and Mum, Bec and a resistant Gus joined Raju in the van to go and secure some important supplies. Gus had quite a meltdown at the prospect of leaving me behind, but twenty kilometres with him on my shoulders was not going to work. As I looked around, the extended team appeared underdressed to walk such a distance. The women were wearing saris and sandals, many of the men had business attire, and there was not a hat in sight. We were much better prepared with our running shoes, special socks, shorts, lycra undershorts, T-shirts, hats and water bladders. On one level this made us feel a bit silly among the crowd, but as the walk day ensued we were happy for every item. I was relieved to see at least Antony had walking shoes. He was one of the special people I met through my work with ChildFund. He was an older Indian man nearing retirement with a big heart and a constant smile. We were all drawn to him and privileged to have him as part of our team. He could talk your ear off with endless research into child development, particularly in the area of nutrition and the use of spirulina, which he believed was an important nutritional supplement for children. In my previous interactions with Antony he had often regaled stories about his beautiful home state of Kerala. I think he was very excited that he was now getting the opportunity to share it with us all.

After an hour of walking we stopped off at a small shop for drinks. It was quite a sight with our team spread out over many benches and steps, and the poor shopkeeper struggling to distribute the water, soft drink and juices to the very thirsty crowd. After several minor arguments about the bill, we were on our way again.

We gradually lost members of our support team as the day progressed. Antony informed us that walking was not something that Indian people liked to do – particularly uphill in such hot weather with sari and sandals. As we made our way out of the urbanised area the landscape slowly changed, and the buildings transformed into tropical green scenery. The walk was predominantly uphill, and although not a steep climb, the slow burn soon made our legs ache. The early laughter and chanting was dying down, and the reality of what it meant to walk over twenty kilometres in a day was dawning on us.

After several hours, the group was in desperate need of some food, so we stopped off at a small restaurant. Mealtime in Indian culture is very important, and the Indian people would never choose to miss a meal. To be honest, the last thing we felt like was a meal. The girls, Nick and I sat out the front with a couple of bananas, a packet of chips and a drink, and took a few minutes to absorb everything. The large group of walkers from ChildFund decided that several hours of walking was enough for them, and they jumped on a bus to head home. They now had a five-hour bus trip home to their village, which they had travelled from to join us for the walk. We said our goodbyes and continued to our designated finish line – the first of over forty. Nick, Indy, Maggie, Antony and myself were the only ones to walk into Kunnamangalam – a far cry from the group of more than sixty walkers that commenced the day. Raju waiting for us with the air-conditioned car was a very welcome sight indeed. We headed back to the hotel for a quick dinner and went to bed feeling very excited about our triumphant first day.

I was so proud of my girls – particularly Maggie, who at only eight years of age walked the whole way in the hot sun. It was hard going toward the end, and to keep her focused we compared this walk to a walk we did back home to give her some perspective. Every now and again I would say to Maggie, 'We're now passing the tennis courts,' or, 'Here we are walking past the school.' It helped keep her focused and moving.

Our first day was beyond our wildest dreams. The walk was now a reality, not only for me but for our entire family. There were many moments on that first day when Indy and I would look at each other and smile, knowing that we were doing something extraordinary, and that our whole family was on board.

Day 5
Kunnamangalam to Pudupatti

That night was tough. Obviously overtired from our first day of walking, Gus was up coughing for most of the night. I probably had an hour's sleep in between taking him to the toilet or to get water or to find dummies. At one point we set up a movie and he found some lollies, which helped to cheer him up. This was at 4 am, mind you. We managed to eventually get back to sleep for another hour or so before I woke sluggishly and with a puffy eye at 7.30 am. Gus woke up full of energy and ready to greet the day, as only a three-year-old can do. This was not the case for the rest of us – Bec and the girls hadn't had much more sleep than I. Jen and Nick headed to breakfast early to order up while we ran around madly trying to get ourselves organised for what planned to be one of the longest walk days of our trip. Our heads felt very cloudy and we were all a little slow. We had breakfast and were excited to see we made it to page three of the *Indian Express* newspaper.

After breakfast Nick, Indy and I left Gus in charge of Mum, Bec and Maggie, and headed off to collect Antony from his hotel. It was a beautiful morning, and we were pleased to be starting our walk earlier to take advantage of the cooler conditions. The Keralan countryside was littered with palms and coconut and banana trees, reminding me of the roads into Noosa. The terrain was quite undulating, and it appeared that we would be walking uphill for most of the day. Along the highway from Kunnamangalam we could see kids playing in the river. I asked Antony why they weren't in school and he informed me that it was Saturday. Another reminder of just how much we had lost track of time and a sense of normality.

Indy was starting to feel the weight of onlookers stares. She was walking in shorts, and the bare legs of a young white girl stand out when many Indian women are covered from head to toe. As we walked, a young man took an interest in our team. Antony shared the story of our journey with him and he seemed very interested. He turned out to be the editor of the local paper, and wanted to do a story on the walk – his photographer would be meeting us at the next town. Antony decided it was a good opportunity to do some impromptu fundraising, and I liked the fact that our walk was receiving financial support not only from people back home but also in India itself. A bucket appeared out of nowhere, and India and Antony walked into shops, sharing our story and securing donation after donation. One man, a visibly poor cobbler sitting by the side of the road, generously donated ten rupees after learning about our cause. Of course in India it is very easy to draw a crowd, and soon many interested onlookers were following us. After an hour or so Indy had raised several hundred rupees, and we found another once in a lifetime experience out of nowhere. We ended up in an open-air bus depot surrounded by a large group of people as Antony thanked his new friend. After the short detour, which took us a couple of hours, we were back to walking.

The sun was getting hotter as we continued the walk, and the cool morning shade and breeze was quickly replaced by harsh sunlight and heat radiating off the bitumen. It must have been well over thirty degrees and quite humid. A little further on we met the girls and Gus, who had been sleeping in the car. Bec jumped out to share a few health warnings regarding walking in such hot conditions, and supplied some hydrolytes. The girls were going to drive on to the next town of Kalpetta, some twenty kilometres away, and secure our lodgings, rather than drive back to the beach. A while after they left us, we received a text from Maggie, saying that is was too dangerous to continue walking. Because Bec hadn't called, we assumed it was nothing and went on. A little further on we saw a nasty traffic accident where a truck had rolled off the road and assumed this was what the fuss was about. Little did we know, up ahead was a road we later named 'Death Road'.

We stopped in a small town for a delicious lunch of kerala parotta and potato curry and a toilet break, which reminded us of the small luxuries of home. The toilet itself was a hole in the ground within a galvanised cubicle outside the restaurant. Later that night, Indy shared demonstrations of the position she had to get into to be able to use the toilet and keep her pants on due to the filth on the ground. She had us all in stitches.

Despite the impromptu fundraising effort, we made good time with our smaller walking group, and so decided to walk beyond our original destination to get to Pudupatti where we stopped for the day by a roadside fruit stall. It had been an extremely long day in difficult, uphill walking conditions. By this stage Indy was well and truly stuffed. Truth told we all were. We had walked over thirty kilometres – the longest walk any of us had ever done. Nick spoke to Bec on the phone, who was still trying to find the accommodation, and she informed us that the terrifying twenty kilometre drive to Kalpetta would take well over an hour. As we sat by the side of the road in the growing darkness waiting for Raju to arrive, we became increasingly anxious about the safety of the girls, as well as how we would go getting up the mountain road ourselves. I was also conscious that Raju had been driving all day in difficult circumstances and was surely getting tired by now.

We imagined what lay ahead of us, trying to make out the Ghat Mountains through the clouds that were now forming. About forty tempos went by in the ninety minutes it took Raju to get back, but at last the big 'TT' found us. Needless to say we were all very relieved. In the van I held tightly onto Indy as we traversed our rollercoaster ride up the mountain; the roads getting narrower and rougher as we went. We weaved our way through hairpin bends, single lane construction sites, buses and trucks in situations you could find on the documentary World's Scariest Roads. Night had fallen, but I could imagine that there was a steep drop off in the darkness beyond the road. On one occasion we came around a corner to find a bus on our side of the road and Raju showed great skill in avoiding a head-on collision. The bus was definitely going to come out as the winner.

The patience of the Indian drivers is amazing. The height of road rage is a flick of the hand, and off they go with little to no aggression – even when we found ourselves in a gridlock traffic jam a kilometre from our lodging. When we eventually arrived at the family stay, we had a catch up with the reunited team, a quick cold meal of delicious parotta and tomato curry – breaking the rule of only eating hot and recently prepared food – and fell into bed for a well-earned night's sleep.

Day 6 Sultan Bathery – forced rest day

Due to the steepness and condition of the road from Pudupatti to Kalpetta, we chose to drive on to Sultan Bathery, the next town, and have a rest day instead of attempting the arduous walk. Truth be told there was no way anyone could walk up that road and we certainly weren't going to attempt it. Maggie and I had awoken with the first hint of Delhi Belly and I was starting to question why I had to break my number one rule about eating in India. Indy, while she appeared to have recovered well from her massive walk the day before, would no doubt benefit from a day off, and the only way that was going to happen was if we all had a rest day. Indy does not have an off switch and if anyone else was walking she would be too.

We farewelled Antony that morning as he had found a ride back to his home in Bangalore. The remaining members of our walking team had a lovely drive from Kalpetta to Sultan Bathery, where we located the Orchid Resort. Don't be fooled by the word 'resort', it was misleading. I think most of the accommodation in India has 'resort' somewhere in the name. We shared a double-room suite, with ample space for Gus to play. The resort was located in a mountain range surrounded in large gumtrees that reminded us of home. There was a small river running along it surrounded by rich green vegetation, and a pool in a colour to match, so unfortunately swimming was once again out of the question. It seemed that pools in India were more for decoration than use; we hadn't found one yet that even slightly resembled the colour blue.

I declined lunch in an attempt to settle my gurgling stomach and put Gus down for a sleep. Lunch was apparently quite calamitous. Mum ended up wearing a plate of vegetable curry that didn't quite make it to the table, and understandably the waiter who dropped it was mortified as she returned to the room to change. One of the boys who worked at the resort was carried past the lunch table after sustaining a fall – bandaged up and looking worse for wear. Nurse Ratchet quickly surveyed the treatment received from the hospital and was not impressed. She once again dived into the first aid kit and rendered some advice and support. Always good in a crisis.

I had the chance to check my emails and saw that we had received the number to call Eibhlin and Nicola – work friends and the next two members of our walk team who had arrived safely in Bangalore. They had been supportive of our cause and we were surprised and excited when they expressed an interest in participating. Both had young families of their own, busy lives and many responsibilities, but saw the opportunity to be a part of an amazing experience and funded their own way to India. I had coached Nicola in Australia in a leadership program, sharing our story and our efforts to support kids around the world. It wasn't easy for her to get involved. She had two boys, and had committed to coming without a great deal of support from home, but worked hard to have the experiences she was craving. As Bec spoke to her on the phone, Gus hunted lizards running up and down a large tree. They were disappearing down a fist-sized hole at its base that resembled a snake hole, so we encouraged the young Steve Irwin to leave it alone. He was not impressed. Given that we had walked past two dead poisonous snakes the day before, we were conscious of the real and present dangers.

Bec headed back to the room to play with her camera, and Gus and I spent a few more minutes surveying the tree. Five boys who worked at the hotel came out and said hi, and Gus very excitedly held court as they hung off his every word. He explained everything from lizard catching, to goat herding. Never one to miss an opportunity, Gus decided to take the boys on a walk, and headed back toward the room. He ran inside to grab his cricket bat and the game was on. Gus took charge and several Indian fieldsmen were very happy to be part of the game – even though their suggestions were quickly dismissed. Gus was in his element, ordering the boys around and taking his turn batting and bowling. Bec, camera in hand, was very excited, and grabbed some beautiful photos of the very natural way Gus and the boys interacted.

After a while I decided to leave Gus to the boys, and headed back to see Bec turning white. While trying to delete one photo from her camera she accidentally deleted all but two. Every day of our trip and every moment that she had painstakingly captured were gone. Panic started, and despite my best efforts to undo her work, it looked like it was too late. Just when all hope seemed lost we remembered the memory stick, and put it in the laptop to check what was there. Relief followed and the colour returned to Bec's cheeks as we could see all the photos saved on a folder, and we moved quickly to make several backups – a good lesson to learn early in our trip.

As the hours passed Maggie and I slowly went downhill and the stomach cramps and pains escalated. Nurse Ratchet was in her element dispensing drugs and treatments left right and centre. It quickly became apparent that it was not going to be an easy night, and after several hours of rest and trying to recover, I was quite violently ill. It was an awful feeling. I didn't know whether I had a twenty-four hour bug or something more serious. On our first trip to India in 1996 Bec caught a bug that took her several months to get over. A bug like that could end the walk for me, and worse if the kids caught it. I was at my lowest, very ill, asking myself what we had signed up for, and worried about Maggie. It is one thing when you are sick yourself but the thought of your kids being sick, particularly so far from home, is very concerning. Fortunately Maggie managed to hold down her antibiotics and recovered quite quickly. In the middle of trips to the bathroom I apologised profusely to Bec for what she was going through, for getting her involved in this ridiculous quest, and saying that we should never have chosen to do this. In usual Bec style she simply said, 'Today is a dark day. Tomorrow will be better.' I knew she was right but I didn't feel that way at the time.

Day 7 Kalpetta to Sultan Bathery – Bec off the bench

After managing to sleep the night before, the day started with another trip to the bathroom and the loss of every drop of water I had diligently sipped through the evening. I had attempted to stay hydrated in a bid to join the walking team, but it soon became clear that this would not be happening. Only a few days into the trip and I had to concede a day's walking. The epic coast-to-coast adventure had produced its first casualty. I lay on the bed and had that awful sensation of the room spinning as I watched the others prepare for the day. Just the thought of a paratha and vegetable curry made me feel sick, so I wasn't sure how I would go for the next five weeks! Bec jumped off the bench and took my place in the team, while Gus rigged up for his second walk effort. They would be walking with Indy and Nick for the twenty kilometres from Kalpetta to Sultan Bathery, while Maggie remained at the hotel with Mum and me. Maggie thankfully awoke asking for food, and spent the day grazing her way through an assortment of meals while showing no signs of cramps. She quickly earned the nickname Iron Guts due to her amazing resilience.

Mum came in to see me somewhat teary and told me how sad she was that I couldn't walk, but I told her not to worry. It was all part of the adventure. There was something very humbling about realising your limitations, of which I have many, and that day showed me again that despite all of our planning and preparations, things can go wrong and the walk had to go on with or without me.

As the hours passed I gradually felt better. A diet of barley sugars and gastrolites seemed to do the trick and despite a whopping headache, I was just happy to be recovering. Maggie and I watched a DVD, relaxed and played cards on the grounds as two of the local ducks looked on. Their antics quickly caught Maggie's attention as they bobbed their heads, and as one stood on the other, she said, 'How cute! They're playing a game.' A quick birds and bees discussion ensued, and Maggie's reply of, 'Oh yuck,' confirmed that she had understood, and indeed was excited about the babies that would come.

Mum left with Raju and the van after an hour to meet the walkers, pick up Gus and get some supplies. They brought back news that all was okay, and stories of elephants and goats. Gus helped himself to French fries and sauce, and then retired for his nap – one he had definitely earned.

A buzz filled the hotel from the energy of the walk crew when they returned after a successful yet tiring day. Bec had completed her first full leg, Nick was resolute, and Indy was pleased with her effort. They headed over for a late lunch as Indy and I enjoyed a game of cards and some dried crackers with Vegemite. She was proving to be an amazing young woman on this trip, and despite my encouragement for her to take extra rest days, she was determined to walk the entire journey. Indy, even at twelve years of age, had a determination and discipline that was quite remarkable. Once she commits to do something she will stop at nothing to reach her goal. She is also quite stubborn, which I have to admit she probably gets from me. Bec agrees. Indy is and has always been the soul of our family, a deep-thinking and beautiful young woman.

As the team settled in for an afternoon rest, Maggie came running in with news of a monkey sighting. Sure enough, there were dozens climbing through the trees surrounding our room. Fortunately they seemed more scared of us than we were of them and fled to the safety of higher ground. Maggie and I followed them down to the river and sat on the steps by the riverbank to watch them feed, feeling a million miles away. We shared a lovely moment, talking about a range of events we had experienced in the recent days. Maggie is a beautiful young girl and the heart of our family. She is a magnet for young children, who run from everywhere to play with her. Fun and light hearted, she is always looking to be around family and friends. She, like her mother and sister, has a set of big brown eyes and a beautiful smile to match.

On the way back we passed Gus in hot pursuit of a few of the young boys from the hotel. They had machetes in hand, ready to burst open coconuts. Gus really shouldn't be getting anywhere near sharp objects, and images of him running like Indiana Jones through the nearby jungle with a machete in hand ran through my head. Even at three the spirit of adventure was alive and well in Gus. Not surprising I guess given his first trip to India was at four months of age, followed by time in East Timor and Thailand, and a six-month trip up the east coast of Australia when he was two. His brief life had already been quite extraordinary. We left the boys to their devices and arrived back at the rooms to hear Mum poking Nick and encouraging him to get out of bed after his afternoon siesta. Gus followed moments later, exclaiming excitedly, 'The boys had a knife. They chopped the coconut. Now where are my jellybeans?'

Just another day in the coast-to-coast adventure.

Day 8

Sultan Bathery to Mysore – welcome and community visit

We awoke to another beautiful morning. The sun was starting to rise above the high coconut trees, and we watched the girls have a quick hit of badminton on the lawn while waiting for breakfast. I was pleased to be returning to a sense of stability as my stomach slowly recovered, even though I wasn't quite ready to face a full Indian breakfast.

On the way back to our rooms, the kids stopped to check in on the two ducks, and on cue, they hopped up to reveal one white egg. If I hadn't known any better, I would have thought it had been planted. Maggie was right after all and don't think she didn't let me know about it!

We packed our bags and jumped in the bus for our hundred-kilometre drive through beautiful countryside to Mysore. Our friends in India advised us – they were too polite to say we mustn't – that this would be an unsafe walk because it ran through a wildlife sanctuary full of leopards and tigers. We agreed. As it turned out, we couldn't have walked through anyway as it was sectioned off by guards and fencing, and every stage of the road had a guard post and roadblock. Unfortunately we didn't see any wildlife, but Raju and the many signposts assured us they were out there.

The drive was uneventful and after several hours we arrived. As we drove in we could feel the increase in population and the buzz that comes with a big city; Mysore is the third largest in the state of Karnataka while the largest is the city of Bangalore. We were only a few kilometres from our hotel when a man on a motorbike stopped next to us at the traffic lights, knocked on the window, and shook his head at Raju to suggest a problem. Worried, Raju looked in his side mirror, turned to us and said, very matter of fact, 'Change of tyre. Thirty-minute delay.' We had since been on the phone to Eihblin and Nicola who informed us they were about to arrive in Mysore by train, and were excited to meet up with them and hear of their Indian adventure thus far.

After our unexpected delay we made it to the Green Hotel; voted one of the best budget hotels in the world partly because it devoted its profits to the local community. It also had a long history of hosting famous authors. Eibhlin and Nicola were waiting for us in the lobby and we all checked in together. It was our third visit to one of our favourite hotels and we felt very much at home. As the staff brought up the extra mattresses, Indy and Maggie informed us that they would be moving into the 'Party Room' with the big girls; evidently in need of some Gus-free time. It was a valid response given his shouts of, 'I don't like you' for most of our day's journey. The little man was showing signs of being just a little over tired.

We contacted our friend, Prem, from ChildFund India, and made arrangements to head to the edge of Mysore for our walk later that day while Gus had a much-needed powernap. Fortunately he woke with an, 'I love you daddy' to confirm his bad mood was behind him, and we drove out to a welcome at Bandipalya – about six kilometres from the Kiriya Pushpa Family Helper Project. Kiriya Pushpa works with approximately 25,000 marginalized families in eighteen urban slums and peri-urban areas surrounding Mysore. The residents are landless day laborers who earn their living through skilled and semi-skilled jobs in construction and the petty trades. Living conditions are poor, and families typically live in small huts or rented concrete houses. Malnutrition is often a contributing factor in child mortality: nearly forty per cent of children under the age of five are underweight. Malaria, tuberculosis, and alcohol abuse among males are also prevalent. Although school enrolment is high, child labor is common. Young girls from migrant families often care for younger siblings or are employed as domestic workers. A small but growing number of children are living on the streets. I was fortunate to visit this community the year before and discuss with them what they believed would be of most help to them. I met with a number of local women who were part of a self-managed support group who spoke on behalf of the community.

We arrived at a major intersection to once again be greeted by ChildFund staff, sponsored children – many of whom I recognised from my visit earlier that year – and female leaders of the local community holding banners with positive messages of our 'walkathon'. There was an excited buzz in the air as the walk team received an official blessing of chalk on our foreheads, a smoke ceremony, and coloured liquid spilt at our feet. Gus almost ended up wearing the lot as he was stuck in his stroller, and the two women holding the ceremony were not always in sync as they swirled the ceremonial liquid around near us.

It was quite a sight to see the now nine members of our walk team and fifty children, staff and volunteers walking on the side of one of Mysore's main roads for much of the eight-kilometre walk through Gunduraonagar along Muneshwaranagar to NIE College Road, until our ending point at the ChildFund project headquarters at St Thomas Church. We all enjoyed the opportunity to walk with and talk to the local families and kids – answering many questions of, 'What is your good name?' and, 'Where are you from?' As we headed to the backstreets, weaving our way through the small streets and decaying houses, we stopped in a range of locations for additional blessings and small ceremonies. Comments between team members focused on how surreal the experience was, and Bec wondered aloud what would we be doing if we were in Australia instead.

There was one young boy named Veeni who took a particular interest in Eibhlin and me. He was very chatty, and told us he was a batsman and a very good dancer. His physical size suggested he was six or seven, rather than his eleven years, which was perhaps due to a lack of nutrition as he was developing. I also saw a lovely young lady I met on my last visit in September, who was studying with dreams of becoming a doctor. We shared our memories of our time together, and I enquired about a sick baby we had met, who had apparently been to the hospital and was now recovering,

After a couple of hours of walking we stopped inside one of the many urban slums around Mysore and the proud home of some of our walking group. We walked into the same small, open hut that my colleague, Jeff, and I visited in September, to see people crammed in from pillar to post. One of the local community leaders commented on how excited everyone was to welcome us to their homes, and suggested that our arrival was akin to the king of Mysore's arrival – much to our embarrassment and the crowd's amusement. The walk team was presented with a rose and a small lemon each and a cake. I lit the candles, and our host cut it and then proceeded to feed each of us, taking great delight in pushing as much cake as she could into everyone's mouths. It was particularly funny watching her shove quite a large piece into Indy's mouth who, while trying to be polite and delicate, ended up with cake across her face. I said a few words, thanking everyone for their generosity and for providing us with such a special experience. This was what the walk was all about.

As the official ceremony finished, we were swamped with handshakes and conversations – Maggie and Indy being particularly popular and seeming to make new friends very quickly. We had tried to reach Mum and Gus – who had spent most of the day with Raju – to meet them on the way, but our message seemed to be getting lost in translation. It was the source of some concern as the last photos were taken and we walked hand in hand with our new friends on our way to St Thomas Church. I was starting to get the hang of traffic patrol duties, and quite confidently strode into open traffic so the entourage could cross safely. As I looked around it was clear that this was another unforgettable moment for the team, with everyone smiling broadly and holding hands with their new friends. I was enjoying watching Nick, an accountant by profession and somewhat by nature, walking along a road in India holding hands with playful children.

We finally made it to our destination as it was growing dark with a group of around twenty people – mainly children. We were very relieved to see Mum and Gus, who had done a great job of entertaining each other in the hot bus all day. I said goodbye to Veeni, who was still holding my hand, and promised to see him on Thursday when he would be dancing for us at a ceremony.

It was very exciting to see firsthand the school kits, water filters and bikes that we had raised funds for at the ChildFund headquarters. We were also informed that we would be supplying emergency treatment for HIV-infected children. It was a great way to finish the day.

Although weary, there was a lot of excited chat on the way home – especially given Gus was updating Raju on his activities of the last hour at ChildFund in great detail. Back at the hotel we washed up for a dinner on the lawn courtyard under a clear, star-filled sky. Gus made friends with Bianca, a young Italian girl. At one stage he had a possie of five girls following him, and entertained them by teaching them how to do cartwheels and forward rolls on the brick paths. We had a lovely dinner, despite our concern for the welfare of the girls that Gus was entertaining, and

I decided to bite the bullet and consume the full curry selection. I couldn't last in India on dry crackers and barley sugars! Gus ate his chicken like it was the first real meal he had had in weeks, when it had only been a matter of days. At that age Gus had an erratic appetite and would often snack his way through the day. We were not precious about this with any of our kids, and ultimately Gus would eat when he was hungry.

Day 9 Rest Day in Mysore

After an emotional and inspiring day of walking, our third rest day was filled with animals and shopping. The morning began with a quick round of greetings between the three rooms, and a sighting of approaching monkeys. The closer they got the more concerned we became – even with our rabies vaccinations the thought of a monkey bite was quite alarming. Maggie spotted one on our balcony, and it was enough to make us retreat to our rooms. They seemed pretty disinterested in us, or at least we thought. I went back into the room to do a couple of things, and next thing I heard Bec on the balcony screaming, 'There's a monkey inside.' Sure enough, I ventured out to our small sitting area from the bedroom to find myself eye-to-eye with a not-too-friendly-looking monkey. He kept his eye on a bag of fruit on our table, and we had a quick stand off while he summed up the situation. He looked at me, I at him. He must have determined that I was of little threat and quickly swiped the fruit bag and made a beeline for the door. Not too quick on his tail, I followed him, and when he dropped it on the way, I seized my opportunity and managed to partially close the door with the fruit inside, and him outside. He still managed to swipe and growl at me, determined to get his fruit, and making a fair racket in the process. By this time Bec and the kids were watching with great interest from the relative safety of their room next door. The monkey eventually gave up, jumped on the balustrade, and continued to growl at me for a while before getting bored and wandering off. Altercation over, I shared the story of how I had wrestled a monkey the size of a gorilla out of our room, and we all headed down to breakfast. On the way we found one of the staff with his slingshot, shooting what looked like fairly soft pellets at the monkeys and encouraging them on their way. So much for the quiet start to the day.

Indy and Maggie headed out with Nicola and Eibhlin to visit Mysore Palace, and came back with stories of riding an elephant – sitting on the head like the real riders do – and surviving another monkey encounter. Indy was also nearly arrested for taking a photo on her smuggled camera, even though phone photography was allowed. I, of course, blamed Eibhlin for leading my daughter astray.

Meanwhile, Jen and Nick went shopping much to Nick's disappointment. Indeed, he fell asleep on the outing, and expressed his desire to return to the road to get on with our walk on multiple occasions. Bec and I took Gus to the supermarket and bought him a scooter. He was demanding a lot of attention, and we thought that a scooter might help him fulfil his insatiable need for activity, while giving us a bit of a break. Needless to say it was a success, and he rode it for hours. We also bought a kettle, which proved just as valuable as the scooter. Up to this point we had been surviving off Mum's handheld element, which boiled one cup at a time, and was proving tiring with Gus's requirement of several 'cup teas' a day.

I took the opportunity to check emails while the girls did some shopping, and got drawn back into technology – easily done in these modern times. I was distracted by a buzzing, and saw a wasp caught in the inside of the window. Now I know I may have exaggerated a little about the size of the monkey, but this wasp was huge. There was no way to open the window to let him out, and with Gus asleep, I had to take my chances and squash him. My first attempts succeeded only in agitating him, but eventually he was subdued. I was glad to see he hadn't invited any friends along. What a day, gorilla wrestling and now wasp hunting and, of course, with no one to witness my bravery!

Although constant horn tooting continued in the background, Bec and I enjoyed a relatively peaceful couple of hours while Gus slept. Travelling with a three-year-old was challenging, and this was a small luxury Bec and I enjoyed each day. Between the constant handwashing, ensuring he wasn't running into traffic, and the need for entertainment, it was exhausting. Bec and I were tiring quickly, but weren't sure how to ask the team for help. I am for the most part an independent person, and as I made the decision to bring our children on the journey, I felt the sense of responsibility to provide all the care they needed. It was still early days, and Bec and I were starting to wonder how we would make it through the rest of the trip.

The girls enjoyed their trip in the autos and came back with a few new things to wear. I think they were thankful for some time out more than anything. Gus awoke ready to party, and the next few hours consisted of taking it in turns to follow him around on his scooter. He particularly liked performing tricks for the other hotel guests and staff, who only served to encourage him by sitting on their balconies and cheering him on. In between scooter trips, he tried to catch frogs in the pond and lizards in the garden, and dodged the bats that came out at night. We had a quick and quiet dinner on the lawns before retiring to our room for a green tea, and the girls to their room for a game of Uno.

A quick calculation showed that while we had been in India for ten days, we had only completed fifteen per cent of our walk. The next leg was six straight days of walking into Bangalore, totalling more than 150 kilometres. We had a community visit the next day, and an opportunity to distribute some of the items purchased with the funds we had raised. It promised to be an amazing day, but we had no idea what was in store for us. As we had become accustomed to in India, we just went along for the ride.

Day 10 Mysore – project visit and an unforgettable day

We headed down to an empty restaurant for breakfast – our chaperone once again keeping the monkeys at bay with his slingshot. As we watched Gus ride his scooter, and Indy show off the rupee she had received from the Indian tooth fairy the night before, we took some time to review our journey so far, and discussed what had and hadn't been working. It was a fruitful conversation that resulted in some good ideas for the next leg. I found the courage to admit we weren't coping with Gus and asked for help. This may seem like a straightforward request, but for a stubborn and pretty independent individual this was harder than it sounded. In a way it was admitting I was failing. I now realise how stupid that sounds, but we men aren't always as bright as we may look. Or perhaps we are. Bec is laughing as I write this so I should probably give up while I'm ahead.

After my plea I had a great response from the team. Eibhlin, Mum and Nick made suggestions, and after that everyone was more proactive in their support for us all, and the trip became much easier.

After breakfast we headed to the Mysore Press Club for a press conference with Prem Kumar from the ChildFund India national office, Father Jonas from the local project we were supporting in Mysore, and around fifteen journalists. Prem was a very happy man, as large as life, particularly popular with Gus, and always there when we needed him. Father Jonas was a quietly spoken man who took charge, and had been very helpful with organising events.

It was our first press conference, and we had no idea what to do or say. Prem and Father Jonas spoke first about our project, and I answered a few questions from the press – some seemed more interested than others in what I had to say. Then it was Gus's turn and once again he was in his element. He started by sharing his thoughts on his goats; much to the delight of the journalists, who just minutes before seemed more interested in checking Facebook than what I had to say. Now Gus had them all eating out of his hand and he carried on sharing a wide variety of stories from the world according to him. All in all the meeting took twenty minutes, and as we were leaving, Bec pointed out the life-size portrait of my inspiration Mahatma Gandhi on the back wall. I felt very much like he was with us in spirit and watching over us. I'm sure he enjoyed Gus's press conference too.

We went to two of the local brick-hut childcare centres that were part of the Kiriya Pushpa Family Helper Project, and funded by ChildFund. We learnt how they, in conjunction with the local project office, worked with the community to identify areas where government programs were not available, and therefore there was a gap in the provision of childcare. These centres allowed parents to leave their children six days a week while they went to work, mostly as labourers, and the children were taught and received nutritious meals and monthly medical checks.

Gus brought along his scooter and put on a show for the kids, and Bec thoughtfully brought bubbles and balls to play with in the small courtyard, which they loved. As always, it was wonderful watching our three interact so naturally and happily with the other kids. The adults were also having a great time. Eibhlin and Nicola loved meeting everyone, Jen and Nick learned a great deal about life for a young child born to a labouring family, and I loved every minute watching the kids play and talking to them. Learning about their lives, challenges and dreams for the future was what the walk was all about. I even brought out my juggling routine, something that I had learned years before when I dabbled in life as a teacher.

After the visits we had a quick thirty minutes back at the hotel before heading out to St Thomas's grounds and the project office. An event had been planned for us to meet children who were going to be the recipients of many of the items we had been fundraising for. Upon arrival, we were greeted by the staff from the project office and the ChildFund India national office – including Antony and Prem. There were also several photographers and another journalist from the *Indian Times* requesting an interview. We couldn't believe the level of attention our walk was getting from the Indian press, and were happy that it was raising awareness about ChildFund India and the many needs of vulnerable children.

When Di Mason first suggested that we could distribute some of the items we had raised funds for, I had an image of us meeting with a local family and presenting maybe one or two bikes. Little did I know what was in store. As we walked behind the project office building and across the school grounds to the presentation, it was apparent that this was going to be an amazing event. We could feel the buzz emanating from the school hall before we even made it into the building. We walked in on a red-carpeted aisle, surrounded by over 500 smiling and cheering children, parents and teachers. It was like nothing I had experienced before.

A large 'Coast to Coast' banner hung behind a set of chairs that were placed on the stage at the front of the hall. Each step felt amazing as we slowly walked up shaking hands and sharing hellos. We all sat on the stage and looked out on the crowd packed in to the rafters. We started with welcome speeches from Father Jonas and Antony and then the show really warmed up. There were traditional and modern dancing from the children, and a few short plays about HIV awareness and children's rights. Indy, Maggie, Gus and I then took turns lighting four candles on the stage. This seemed easy enough until Gus started blowing them out as fast as we could light them. Despite nearly causing chaos we got there in the end; it just took a little longer than anticipated.

I could tell from the looks on the faces of my family and friends that they were as overwhelmed as I was by what we were experiencing. It was amazing to go from expecting to see a couple of families to being a part of a major production, no doubt many weeks in the planning. Even the Bishop of Mysore joined us. At one point he and Maggie were having a nice old chat. I would have loved to hear what they were talking about – it is always hard to know with Maggie. She was probably sharing her opinion on his outfit.

Then came the moment we had been working toward for the last fifteen months – presenting the children with their items. First, India presented brand new bikes to sixty girls who approached the stage one at a time. Some of these girls had been walking up to six kilometres to school each day, which was time–consuming, difficult, and unsafe.

Secondly, we presented new schoolbags and kits to over a hundred orphaned children, ranging from three-year-olds to teenagers. I took every chance I could to kneel down and look into the eyes of these grateful kids.

Gus stood at the front of the line and handed over the schoolbags full of school supplies and shook the hand of every child. I looked over to see Bec crying quietly and sat down next to her. It was such a special moment for us to share. Eibhlin then distributed her water filters for the local schools, so that the children would have access to clean drinking water.

By this stage the kids were overexcited and rapidly losing concentration. In a bid to entertain them for just a little longer, Gus – who had sat patiently watching the other children perform all day – cartwheeled and rolled across the stage, and I accompanied him with a short speech. His persistent questioning of, 'When will it be my turn?' had finally paid off. As the Gus Show continued, I valiantly attempted to say something meaningful. I talked about the right every child has to grow up in a safe and healthy environment, and be able to go to school, and that we wanted to live in a world where this is not an aspiration, but a reality. I shared our experience of the warm and friendly hospitality we always experienced when in India, and our two favourite quotes: 'No one can do everything, but everyone can do something', and, 'Be the change you want to see in the world'. I mentioned that the people in the hall would probably never truly understand how special it was to experience the difference our contributions would make firsthand. I thanked them for allowing us to be a part of the day.

I then handed the microphone to India who provided an inspired talk about the impact this experience was having on her life, and how grateful she was to be involved, followed by a few heartfelt words from Maggie.

Gus, having waited impatiently through all of this, took another opportunity to shine and was off, with one hand on his hip and the other on the microphone. He talked about goats, helping kids, and his favourite Indian Raju. The list was endless and he had the entire crowd hanging off every word. Indy and Mags, who were not so taken with being shown up by their three-year-old brother, luckily gave him the wind up, otherwise he would probably still be talking now. After our presentation the Bishop of Mysore gave a moving talk, including his appreciation for the work we were doing. Following on from him was another highlight of the day – dancing from Veeni and his team. It was a spectacular performance. Look out Bollywood!

After a few final words of thanks the presentation was over, and we adjourned to the school grounds for tea as the sun was setting. Veeni presented Eibhlin and me with a touching gift that he had organised of his own accord. While benefiting from community programs and sponsorships, he had not yet been sponsored himself. We were experiencing firsthand the impact that ads for sponsoring children just like Veeni made. Sponsorship can make an enormous difference not only to kids but also the communities they live in.

Gus took off on his scooter, which was hard to manoeuvre on the grass, so I found a small concrete area for him to practice his moves where I could still watch the other kids playing. There were girls proudly riding their new bikes, and children wearing their schoolbags – some of them dwarfed in comparison. I took a moment to think about how far we had come from our conversation in Barwon Heads Caravan Park fifteen months earlier.

We had collectively raised over A$60,000, met wonderful people, and had hopefully encouraged others to make their contribution to this world. Remember, everyone can do something.

As the sky grew darker and the day drew to a close, most of us fell back in the bus with a sense of euphoria. Unfortunately the same could not be said of Gus, who – after a very busy day and having missed his afternoon nap – had one of the biggest meltdowns we had experienced; yelling, 'I don't like you' and, 'Don't look at me' slightly more often than we were used to.

Indy was having an equally as emotional time as she looked back on the day. She was at an age where she really understood what we were trying to do as a family, and what we were achieving. After lots of tears – which is quite rare for Indy – a chance to express herself, lots of cuddles and a wash, she was off next door to play Uno for who got the beds with Nicola and Eibhlin. The winners each night got to sleep in the beds, and the losers had to sleep on the mattress on the floor. Meanwhile, Gus had calmed down enough for a cuddle, and told me that he didn't like it when people pinched his cheeks. It turned out that once again that too many people had surrounded him, and he was scared and overwhelmed. In case we needed it (and we shouldn't have) Gus reminded us that he needed to feel safe when we were at these events, and we promised that it wouldn't happen again. He had two cups of tea and went to bed.

The rest of the team enjoyed a communal debriefing and dinner downstairs, while I preferred a moment of quiet reflection as I ate a bowl of noodles and typed up my blog. We all had our own ways of drawing inspiration and joy from our experiences.

I am not sure I can do justice to that day. I hope that those of you who donated to our cause can understand the difference you made. If only you could have seen the faces of the kids as they received their much-needed items and heard their words of thanks. It was an unbelievable experience and I felt numb all over.

Day 11 Mysore to Srirangapatna

We received word from my sister Kate that her kids, Alice and Max, and their schools – St Mary's Memorial and Westminster College – had raised A$1500 for our cause. Ally had a casual day and gave an inspiring talk to her schoolmates, while Maxy organised a walkathon – very fitting – from Glenelg to Somerton in Adelaide. It gave us a real buzz to know there were still people back home interested in what we were doing and supporting us, and given the events of the day before, we were even more aware of the opportunities this money would create.

We had planned a 9 am start so were up early for breakfast; all dressed in our green ChildFund T-shirts. We were now affectionately known among our team as 'Team Green' or 'Team Irish'. Eibhlin, if you hadn't already guessed, was from Ireland. She had such an impact on Indy that our girl started talking with an Irish accent. Not a word here or there, but a total accent change. Eibhlin ran ultra marathons as a hobby, was as tough as nails and a wonderful role model for our daughters. She also supported Bec on the walk, and made it her personal goal to help her relax and enjoy herself, which Bec greatly appreciated.

I had slept poorly the night before due to the emotion of the day and the bright lights shining into our room, but could still appreciate the palpable energy of the team. We headed off with Raj to meet at St Theresa's church; our lunch of peanut butter and Vegemite sandwiches safely packed away. On the way I asked Bec if she knew where my sunglasses were – they weren't in their usual spot on top of my hat. She pointed out that they were, in fact, already on my face. It was going to be a long day.

We arrived at the church to a sea of smiling, positive faces. Prem and Anthony greeted us, and we spotted Father Jonas, Vincent, and various other ChildFund staff. There was no strict plan, other than to protect Gus and his cheeks. Antony, after his impromptu fundraising effort in Kerala, decided to try again with another fundraising walk, consisting of two groups with green buckets and ChildFund flyers to distribute through the streets of Mysore. The majority of people we approached were very happy to support the cause, particularly when the kids asked. Maggie, especially, was a natural.

Amid the slow walk, there were the usual engrossing moments that India provided: a calf stood on the main road, and a bus screeched to a halt and gently nudged it on its way; Gus asked why the thing hanging in the butcher's window had a tail and an interesting conversation followed, given his love of goats; but the most confronting sight was two legless men, witnessed at different times of the morning, pulling themselves down the road through the traffic. A poor person with a significant disability in India rarely gets access to the resources they need, and are left to cope as best they can. It once again made us question what we have to complain about, and gave us some perspective.

What really surprised me was the contradiction of those who had the most to give often giving very little or nothing at all. And vice versa; those who clearly had very little were happy to contribute what they could. We approached tourists who were interested in our cause, but would ignore us when we asked for a donation. Then we met people staying with us at the Green Hotel, who had seen our story in the paper, and made a very generous donation. The contrasts of the human condition were inescapable. I learned (or was learning) not to judge or compare, but to accept. I had found that it was an easy trap to fall into. Instead, I tried to focus on what I could do, and not worry about what I couldn't change. This lesson is still sinking in!

The long morning was very successful for ChildFund, but the five kilometre fundraising walk took three hours to complete, and left us exhausted. We were the first group to get to the meeting place at a major roundabout in central Mysore, and waited half an hour for the others to arrive. On my mind was the fact that it was now nearing the hottest part of the day, and we still had fifteen kilometres to walk. We stood in the shade and watched as every vehicle imaginable, as well as hundreds of pedestrians, worked their way around the five-road intersection. At one point the traffic was stopped and an old, barefoot man covered head to toe in dirt, and wearing just an old shirt, shorts, and a cloth wrapped around his head, came into sight. He walked around the roundabout in the middle of the three lanes, pulling a small wagon behind him. Next minute the lights changed, and scooters, motorbikes, autos, cars, trucks and buses swamped him. Not to be perturbed, the old man kept walking, and the traffic made its way around him. Only in India.

Soon the other group came into sight, and together we celebrated the estimated 10,000 rupee collected and the awareness we had raised. It was subdued, however, by the confusion regarding Eibhlin's whereabouts. Someone suggested that she had gone back to the hotel with Nicola, Maggie, Mum and Gus, although we didn't see her. A few calls later and we were still none the wiser. It was past 1.30 pm and we were growing increasingly anxious. Finally, out of the crowd popped Eibhlin, bucket in hand, doing her bit for ChildFund.

The highlight of the morning was when one of the girls from the day before stopped by on her new bike to thank the group for her gift. It was wonderful to see our actions making such a difference, and so quickly.

After a quick Vegemite sandwich and a round of goodbyes, we walked with Father Jonas to the edge of town where he sent us on our way. After this the walk was quite uneventful but pleasant thanks to the milder conditions. We made our destination by 4.30 pm, very happy with our efforts. Raju, as if on cue, arrived to collect us to take us back to Mysore.

The day had taken its toll on an exhausted Indy, who could only be convinced to come down for dinner after a cry, a cuddle, and a wash. The evenings were quite cool out in the grassed courtyard, and dinner there by candlelight was one of the treats of the Green Hotel. Eibhlin ordered up for the table, Gus scooted around catching lizards and frogs with Nicola's help, and we enjoyed a lovely dinner to mark our final evening in Mysore.

Day 12
Srirangapatna to Mandya

Breakfasts were becoming a little more pedestrian as our trip continued; cornflakes with banana and milk, and toast with jam or fried eggs. After my stomach scare I was happy for the change. We were able to convince Indy to have a rest day. The fact I had missed a day as well made it easier to coerce her, as she could see it was something we would all require. Maggie took her big sister's spot, and joined the ever-reliable Nick, Nicola – who would be walking her first full day –and myself. A quick check of the itinerary revealed it was going to be one of our longer walks at twenty-six kilometres.

Around ten minutes after leaving Srirangapatna, Maggie began the 'how much longer' game. It was clearly going to be a long day. We walked down a small dirt track with little houses on either side – eager to get off the main road – and were immediately surrounded by the local kids, who were very pleased to see us. We got the feeling that not too many westerners would visit here. A woman carrying a pail of water soon stopped us. Her face beamed as she introduced herself as Celia in broken but understandable English. She gestured to her house just down the road, and we immediately took up her offer to see it. Her bed took up most of the main area, and a small divider separated another makeshift room with a bed for her two adult sons. She pointed out the shelved walls, which allowed the house to double as a shop. It was very humbling to see how her family lived, and even in spite of her lack of material wealth, she gave Maggie and Nicola a range of goods and refused payment. After multiple attempts, Nicola was eventually able to force rupees into her hand.

Further up the road we came across a school, which was – much to Maggie's disgust – filled with kids on a Saturday. I don't think she could fathom it! They were clambering and hanging out of windows, very excited to share their work with us. We spent some time with them, but needing a place to rest, set off again and found a small place for our morning coffee, with Maggie eagerly joining in. While there, we met Manjunath – the manager – who had seen our story in the paper. He was from Hubli, a town around 600 kilometres away, and had left his wife and young daughter behind, having come to work in the town for financial reasons. He missed his family, and shared his excitement about seeing them in a few days when he would return home. He was excited to hear we were Australian, and said that he liked Steve Waugh and Ricky Ponting. As we were leaving, he pushed a book in my hands – a gift from one of his friends. We wished him well, thanked him for his generous gift, and continued our walk.

The road we found ourselves on could easily have been

any country road in Australia: a dual carriageway, gum trees, and dusty verges. As we walked, and I pulled Maggie up the hill, a man walking his bike came up alongside us. His name was Chinderal, and he had grass cuttings for his two oxen. He spoke a little English, but often just talked in his local language as though we understood what he was saying. He shared with us that he was not yet married, and that would be happening next – whatever that meant. He offered us to come to his village, but we gratefully declined, and as we had made it to the top of the hill, he jumped on his bike and said goodbye.

After nearly three hours walking Maggie was finding each step a challenge, as you could imagine any nine-year-old would. We found a small roadside mound in the shade and stopped for a sandwich and a rest. It was now midday and we were expecting the vehicle any minute so Maggie could catch a ride back to the hotel. Much to her disappointment, the support team was out shopping when we called. She rallied, however, when we started talking about Jasper – our new puppy in waiting – and continued a one-sided conversation for the next ninety minutes. She set a cracking pace, and we soon left Nick and Nicola in our tracks. The support crew finally arrived, and after our hellos, health checks and topping up of water supplies, Maggie jumped into the air-conditioned car, very happy with her efforts. Having had a minute to rest, she decided she wanted to finish the days walking. This is the same girl who was asking ten minutes in to the day when she could get picked up, if there was an auto we could ride in, where Raju was, if we should try hitchhiking, if she could jump into an oxen wagon. And now after twenty kilometres she was looking to finish the walk. What a super effort from our little nine-year-old adventurer.

Thinking we only had three kilometres left for the day we set off – Indy joining us for the final leg, refreshed after her restful morning. After a few kilometres Maggie turned to me and said, 'My knee feels like it's having childbirth.' Fortunately, in the distance we could see a town, and as we got closer the Hotel Jyothi International appeared like a mirage, and we spotted Mum, Bec, Eibh and Gus waiting for us. We had made it. As it turned out, the final stretch was closer to five kilometres, which brought the days total up to twenty-six kilometres in nearly six hours.

Our $30 a night hotel turned out to be a pleasant surprise, and we relaxed and swapped stories over a cold coke and packet of Lays potato chips. Having spent the day with her new idol, Eibhlin, Indy continued to develop her hybrid Aussie/Irish accent, and used it to inform us that Nicola exhausted from her day, didn't see the shower, and proceeded to wash with the small hand-held hose usually reserved for the washing of one's butt. Eibhlin informed me that Indy, after all of this, also decided to use the butt washer as it turned out to be warmer than the shower. When in India! Maggie and Indy were sleeping with Nicola and Eibhlin again, and went to their rooms to watch *Twilight* on the laptop. Nicola and Maggie lasted about ten minutes before they crashed.

Day 13 Mandya to Maddur

The night before had once again been a little unsettled, between bright lights being shone into our room, to a wayward mosquito net, to Gus going to the toilet and asking for a cup of tea at some ungodly hour. We woke early that morning as we had committed to a 7 am breakfast. It was straight into preparations.

We were the first to line up for breakfast and most of us decided to go for omelettes, bread, pineapple juice, and coffee. The omelettes came out wrapped around the bread, something we had not encountered before. The highlight that morning was being able to start our walk directly from our hotel, which wasn't something we'd previously had the opportunity to do. The walk team was Nick, Eibhlin, Indy, Bec and myself. Nanna and Nicola generously agreed to be on Gus duty to allow Bec a rare and cherished walk opportunity.

We did our homework and in a bid to spend more time away from the main road, chose a track that ran between it and a railway line. We felt the benefit and beauty of walking past the farmers and families washing by the river, preparing their breakfasts, and doing chores. The peace and quiet was lovely after days of screeching buses and tormenting truck horns.

After a while we came across a small township and found ourselves walking through the butchers' quarters. Every second shop had a carcass of some description hanging in the window. It sounds worse than it was. Eibhlin thought it smelled like her dad's cow yard.

Everyone was again extremely friendly, with a seemingly constantly flow of:

'Hi.'

'How are you?'

'Fine.'

'Where are you from?'

'Australia.'

The local kids especially thought that we were very funny walking by in our outfits.

After the butchers' courtyard I spotted an Indian barber shop consisting of two chairs crammed into a small yellow room, and gestured to the group that it was time. Since the beginning of the trip I had been looking to get a very short haircut for the first time, an idea that the kids were against. Nick also wanted a trim to get back to his near-bald state. He was up first, and sat next to a man who was having his sideburns blackened with a toothbrush. As you can imagine, we were creating quite a buzz in the morning air of this small country town, and starting to draw a crowd of interested onlookers. Before the barber was finished with Nick he gave him a coating of baby powder, which had him, in Nick's own words, 'smelling and looking like a baby's bum'.

Then it was my turn. Indy ran her fingers through my hair one last time, with obvious trepidation about my choice. I asked for a number two on the razor, hoping that meant something to my friendly barber. Unfortunately the power cord plug kept slipping out of the wall and turning the clippers off. Every time they stopped, they pulled a small clump of hair with them. In the end the barber called for reinforcements to hold the plug in. At that stage the back of my head was clipped, but there was still a nice little bird's nest on top. I wondered what would happen if the clippers died. Meanwhile, the girls were having a great laugh watching and filming the procedure. A few minutes later and I was a new man, complete with a baby's powder covering. Indy was in shock, but Bec liked it. We paid $2 for the two cuts, had photos with our barbers, and thanked them for their wonderful service.

We continued through the town and out the other side past the impressive local sugar factory, which, according to the locals, was a major attraction. We watched trucks back wheel-deep into the water for their Sunday wash at the river as Bec stopped for her first bush wee of the trip. While chaperoning her, Eibhlin stood on a prickle bush, and we spent some time pulling the centimetre-long thorns out of her shoes. Luckily no damage was done.

We continued along the railway line, sheltered by sugar canes and other crops, until it disappeared and we crossed the railway tracks to walk along a grassed area. Two oxen-led wagons soon caught up to us, and we stepped aside to let them pass. Indy was hoping for a ride, but one look at their load of manure changed her mind. There we were in rural India, following two wagons full of manure to a town called Maddur. The humour of that situation was not lost on our team.

For a short time we were forced to walk along the tracks, but luckily no trains came, and we soon came across a grassy path that seemed like a superior alternative. Nurse Bec warned everyone to stay vigilant and gave us a run down in the event of a snakebite. I was in my own little world, having a Gandhi moment, and looking for a staff to walk with. We had been walking for a few hours so I wasn't very sharp, and clearly wasn't listening to Bec as attentively as I should have been. I looked down and saw what I thought was a reasonably large part of a stick, and I was about to grab it when it started moving. I jumped about six feet in the air, Eibhlin swore, and Nick started screaming, 'What is it? What is it?' Sure enough, the stick was a snake, and we had our first reptilian encounter. It had the best possible result, however, given there was a warning but no contact, and it disappeared immediately. All of our hearts were pounding and our eyes certainly began to take notice of the grass ahead.

We soon came to a small collection of farmhouses that felt more like someone's backyard than a village. Bec started questioning my navigational skills, which was probably fair enough. We noticed a motorbike slowly making its way along a narrow path through the fields, and saw the main road just beyond that, so I was able to convince the team that we were heading in the right direction. Women and children greeted us as we walked past, and in the yard of one house we noticed three colourful tombstones.

My questionable navigation only seemed to worsen as the path we were on disappeared to make way for paddy fields. At the recommendation of a young lady walking her cow, and after a quick team discussion, we decided to risk it and press on through the fields. The initial section went smoothly, but we soon came to a path half a metre in width, lined with sugar canes. We looked back and the lady was still gesturing us on. There was now a fifty-metre stretch in front of us, which we affectionately named Snake Alley. Given our encounter only an hour before, we proceeded

Preparing the supplies – must have Vegemite! This was the case for the food (you should have seen the medical case). It was really stressful trying to fit everything in. There were tears all round.

Adelaide airport – the adventure begins, a moment of relief after the stressful lead-up. After take-off I indulged in a decent gin and tonic.

Start of our walk in Khozhikode: there's no turning back now – an overwhelming thought given the journey ahead of us.

Ceremonial blessing for Gus in Mysore, complete with cheek pinching. I wonder what he was thinking about all this.

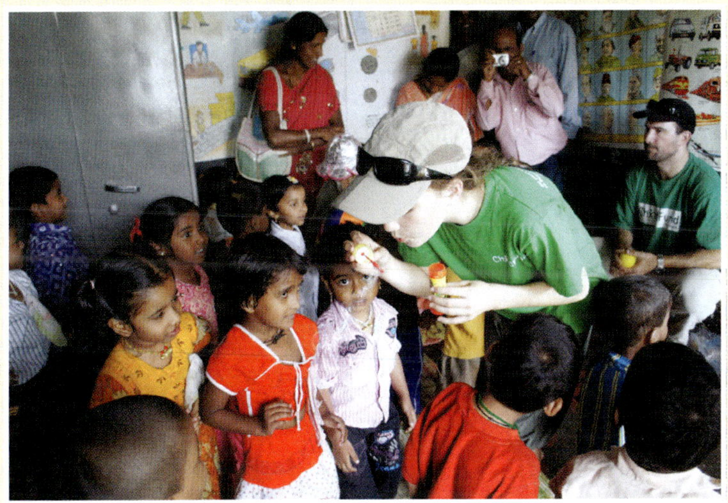

Kiriya Pushpa child-care centre, an amazing ChildFund project that enables the poorest families to work full-time while their children receive an education, nutritious meals and medical care. We loved hanging out with the kids bubble blowing, juggling and scooter riding.

Indy and Maggie were welcomed like rock stars at our community visit in Mysore. Our hosts insisted on feeding the cake in our honour to Indy and Mags.

The most emotional reception of our walk. We had this crazy idea that we would just fly to India, enjoy meeting the children, and fly out without being noticed. At our first community reception, complete with red carpet and over 500 people, we quickly realised we might attract a bit more attention.

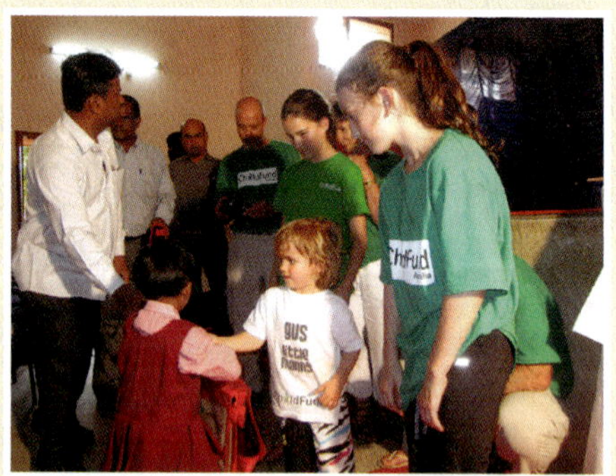

Gus presents an orphaned girl from the Kiriya Pushpa Family Helper Project with her new school kit. Even though Gus was only three, I believe this experience will have a positive impact on him.

Gus and the Pope of Mysore share a joke at our gift-giving reception in Mysore.

Time for a change! The two Nicks get their heads shaved by the 'Arturo Tavernas' of India, a hilarious experience. Once the barbers got over the shock they were excited – and I think our visit was good for business.

Following the manure to Maddur – literally! This was one of those only-in-India moments.

The walk Channapatna to Bidadi, sharing rural southern Indian roads with goats and goatherders. We're all accidentally colour coordinated!

An emotional family reunion at Bangalore International Airport, 23 December 2011. For Kate and her kids, a first trip to India. From left to right: Max, Indy, Ally, Kate, Maggie, Gus, Nick, Big Nick and Jen.

The family, with our trusty Tempo Traveller in Bangalore, driven by our wonderful driver, Raju. The Tempo Traveller was like the mirage in the desert for the kids at the end of a long, hot walk day and, if I'm honest, for the adults too!

Bucket collecting, not a favourite! The kids put on a brave face. They would spend hours walking shop to shop asking for donations from local business owners. What blew me away was the generosity of the Indians, even those with little wealth. In fact those who refused to donate tended to be white tourists!

Roadside blessing on the road from Bethamangala to Bangarapet. Young girls would bless us, place a bindhi on our forehead, and present us with beautiful fragrant garlands, which were surprisingly heavy!

The faces of these children from the Kolar community school are just so radiant and beautiful. Here are children who have so little, yet seem much happier than many of our own with all their possessions.

En route to community visit in Bangarapet. We could not believe the crowd that that joined us for our walk, even a local politician of sorts.

Ally had some dedicated followers on her way to our Bethamangala community visit. The Indian girls loved to learn all about these fascinating Aussie teenagers.

Maggie was a source of great interest to these young ladies on the road to Bethamangala. Luckily Maggie loves to chat.

Local school visit in Kolar community. The kids are always immaculately presented, their uniforms spotless and wrinkle-free, their hair perfectly groomed. Children here felt very fortunate and privileged to attend school; I was secretly hoping that some of their enthusiasm might rub off on my kids.

Walking into the cyclone heading to Chennai. A really tough walk day, it was actually cold, which you would think a blessing, but it was a damp, blister-inducing miserable cold. Many people offered us a ride on their bike, cart, or truck and seemed perplexed when we declined. I can only imagine what our passers-by in this photo must be thinking.

A much-needed roadside coffee stop to re-invigorate the crew as we headed toward cyclonic Chennai. Even the kids enjoyed this milky sweet specialty coffee.

A special reunion with our dear friends, Subashini (centre, blue dress) and Christopher (far left), outside their family-owned business, the K Paul Hotel RUHSA. We were last there in 1996 when Subashini was a schoolgirl, Christopher about 8, and the K Paul Hotel an open hut.

Bucket bathing, the next best thing when the risk of swallowing water from showering is too great. All I have to do now is work out how to tackle the dreadlocks!

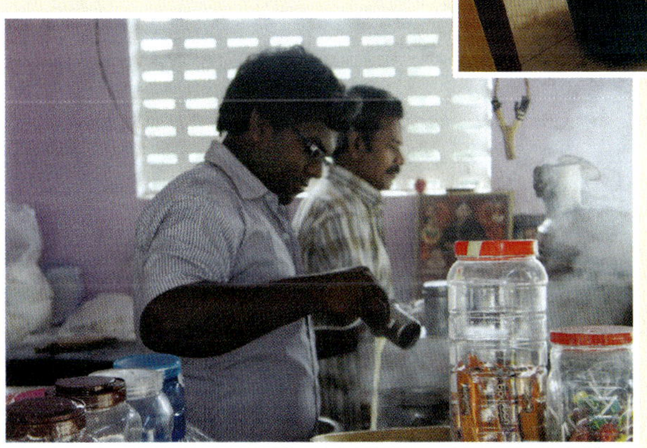

Christopher and Paul making us a famous South Indian coffee at their restaurant, K Paul Hotel.

The old and the young! Gus exploring lanes in rural RUHSA.

On the walk from Ranipet to Kaveripakkam, Gus closely studies the children, earnest in prayer, before lunchtime at a local primary school. He was then quickly back on his scooter showing off his moves and teaching the kids a few tricks too.

Filming day in Ranipet provoked some anxiety for our kids. The local kids loved it!

Ally, Indy and Max handing over to children of the KKSS community in Chennai the bikes purchased with the funds they raised. It was a bit scary to watch the girls proudly cycle away as many of them had never ridden a bike before.

Day 33 and 65 kays to Chennai, which felt like 65 too many at this stage. It had been very hot, dry, noisy and dusty walking with lots of roadside ablutions to dodge.

Nick chats with kids in Chennai, excited to receive their new school kits. They received their kits wearing their usual serious, polite little faces, but once out of sight they were all smiles, happily inspecting the contents.

Kate gets clucky at the Gypsy community visit. It made me stop and think about how differently we raise our children in Australia. I felt gratitude mixed with a degree of shame and embarrassment at our often sterile, over-cautious approach.

Big Nick is welcomed like royalty with handmade signs from the kids at the Gypsy community visit. We were used to the poverty and primitive living conditions in India, but this surpassed all we had seen. Encouraging these nomadic people to settle was a major and challenging project for ChildFund.

Maggie makes friends with these children at the Gypsy community.

We made it! Exhilarated after six weeks and more than 800 kilometres, we hit the warm waters of Marina Beach, Chennai.

A poignant and emotional family moment at the end of our journey as we stand beneath our inspiration, Mahatma Gandhi, each of us contemplating the enormity of what we had achieved.

WALKING FOR A CAUSE

Walkathon: Aussie Family Distributes Largesse

A walk to remembe

ily walks to give

I WANTED TO DO SOMETHING FOR THIS NATION AND DECIDED TO RAISE MONEY TO HELP THE NEEDY CHILDREN

Walkathon

Oz family on a mission

Walking coast to coast for a cause

Australian family on walkathon for welfare of poor children

A Walk from Kozhikode to Chennai for a Noble C

lkathon for children's cause

The campaign is to raise funds for the education of poor children in south India.

Media collage put together by our friends at ChildFund. We couldn't believe the attention our adventure attracted but we were very happy to use it to promote the amazing work of ChildFund.

quite tentatively along the narrow path. I was now the most experienced with snakes, and clearly dubbed the least important by the rest of the group, so I went first, closely followed by Eibhlin, Indy and Bec, with Nick bringing up the rear. We were silent and anxious, so Nick began to sing an old favourite family song. As we nervously continued, the voices slowly started ringing out – 'Tintinara kicks forward, forward, forward, Tintinara kicks forward' – to take our minds off the Snake Alley of Death.

Before we knew it we were out and found ourselves next to a service station on the main road. We had a quick toilet and Vegemite sandwich stop. Indy expressed her disregard for the toilets, which Eibhlin reinforced, saying in her classic Irish accent, 'the toilet paper was too good for that toilet'. It wasn't the most glamorous spot to stop, but we all needed a short breather after traversing Snake Alley. We reluctantly decided to stay on the main road to finish off the day, and pushed out the last ten kilometres in good time. Eventually we came to a sign welcoming us to Maddur and stopped for our celebrations, team photos, and the usual soft drinks and chips. As if on cue, Raju pulled up to collect us as we were finishing.

The staff set up a long table for us in the middle of the car park – given the brick huts designed for meals were restricted to parties of six – and we dined under the stars as the occasional bat flew by. Gus was able to ride his scooter while we enjoyed a relaxing evening. Nicola and Mum shared stories from their day. They had ventured out to a local community with Gus to visit a few families and see their homes. It sounded like they, too, had a great day.

Day 14 Maddur to Channapatna

Eibhlin, Maggie, India, Nick, and I had twenty kilometres to walk for our fourteenth day. We again decided to head off the main road, and followed the railway line like the day before. We walked through the backstreets, past houses, and interacted with kids as they got ready for school. We spied a stray mongoose running through a field, which was a little concerning given one of their main food sources is cobra. Passing through an industrial section, we saw large factories taking chunks of granite the size of cars and slicing them down to thin, benchtop size slabs. Maggie sang her way through the morning, much to Indy's annoyance and Eibhlin's amusement.

Indy was a little flat – the singing wasn't helping – so I encouraged her to join Raju on the bus. Meanwhile, Maggie had a spring in her step after spotting a sign to a McDonalds up ahead. The kids didn't go to McDonalds very often, but the thought of something familiar was clearly very energising. She picked up the pace and practiced her order as we walked. The bus found us a little way up the road and we decided to do a changeover. Very reluctantly, Indy and Maggie stayed with Raju for some McDonalds and a rest, and Nicola – who was still a little sore from her mammoth twenty-six kilometres in one day – joined the team. I was pleased that Indy relented and was prepared to manage her limits. She was defiant at the start of the trip, and had been determined to walk every step.

The rest of the day was quite uneventful, and we covered more than our original distance by around 1.30 pm. We made it to the town of Channapatna, and, as the others were finding it hard to locate our accommodation for the evening, we decided to press on. The town was quite large and centred around a bus station. It was very hot and dusty by this time, and it was a great relief when we made it to the open road. After a few kilometres Raju managed to find us. It was time to call it a day.

Our accommodation was interesting – the word I use when no other label seems to apply. Twenty years ago it could have been a mecca, but when we visited it looked like a run-down ghost hotel. There was an unfilled swimming pool, various tired recreation areas, rabbits and turkeys in the gardens, and a leisure bar and café; neither looked like they had been used in years. The rooms were large but very uninspiring, and every square metre seemed to contain a mothball. The girls decided to bunk in with Nicola and Eibhlin again, so they took the larger room. Jen and Nick were in another, and Bec, Gus and I had the third.

After a walk around the grounds we had some dinner – vegetarian was the option of choice – and then called it a night. Nick and Indy were coming down with colds, and we were not sure who would make the walk the next day. We were four days into a six-day stretch, and the physical challenge was starting to become a reality.

Day 15 Channapatna to Bidadi

As often happens I awoke a little earlier than Bec and Gus, and took some time to think about our journey so far. I also thought about losing Tim. At my lowest times in the lead up to the walk when I lacked confidence and doubted my ability, Tim pushed me forward, and helped me build commitment to our journey. I drew inspiration from him every day of our trip.

We were over two weeks into our six-week journey, and the kids had been fantastic the whole time. They had been engaged, fun and motivated. Indy had been a strong and committed member of the team, fully immersing herself in every opportunity, and taking a great deal from her interactions with the various communities. She was a credit to herself, and I was in awe of her every day. Maggie brought her humour and her unique ways. Despite winning the award for least organised member of the team, she was a strong and resilient nine-year-old, who proved that she was up to some major physical challenges. There are not too many kids that age who have walked twenty-six kilometres across rural India in one day. She was also a very positive member of the team, who loved interacting with people and situations around her, and was very popular with other kids . She sung her way through life, and when she got in the Maggie Zone she would talk your ear off without stopping for breath. Gus had been a little legend. He loved everyone he met, and interacted freely with adults and children alike. He had his meltdowns and tantrums as any three-year-old would, but we were still so thankful to have him every step of the way.

My mum maintained a positive attitude despite a couple of testing events along the way. She was also extremely helpful with Gus, and stepped up to allow Bec to be a part of the walk and relax knowing that he was in good hands. Nick was, as he always has been, our rock. He moved between this no fuss, get on with the job attitude, to a fun-loving, song-singing, storytelling entertainer, whom the kids adored. Nicola and Eibhlin had also been wonderful. They were on their first trip to India, and came open to the experience with no expectations. I find people can have two opposing experiences in India – I personally have had both. Some people hate it. They can't wait to leave, and never want to return – often because don't stay long enough to get over the initial shock. Others think that India is a magical place; full of wonderfully contrasting experiences of people and culture, and every sense is stimulated in some way. Nicola and Eibhlin, fell into this latter category, and loved every minute of their trip. They were amazing with the kids, and it was energising to have them as part of both the walk team and the support crew.

Finally to my courageous and beautiful wife Bec, who was the soul of our family, and a woman who inspired us all in her subtle and unassuming way. I have always said that Bec brings sunshine everywhere she goes, and people warm to her as a result. While I am the quieter, more reserved type, who shies away from the crowd, Bec is the consummate host, bringing people together and making sure everyone is okay. She had been the queen of answering 'where's my …' and stayed calm while tending to the many requirements of the team. She was our organiser, our supporter, our nurse, and our friend. I couldn't have asked for more. We had come a long way together, and I loved spending each and every day with her.

We were in day five of six long walking days, and with a cold going through the team, the kids decided to take a well-earned rest. Nicola, Nick, Bec and I left Mum and Eibhlin on support crew duties, and headed off for our twenty-six-kilometre walk from Channapatna to Bidadi.

That morning, I did something I had committed never to do and got involved in a family dispute. That is, another family's dispute. We had just stepped out of the vehicle to start walking, and could hear a child crying. The noise was coming from beside a nearby vehicle, where a boy of around five years of age, dressed in school uniform, stood screaming. A man stepped out of the vehicle, and raised the stick clutched in his right hand in preparation to hit him. I started to walk toward the pair of them before he had a chance to do so, watching intently. As soon as the man noticed me, he hid the stick, and grabbed the sobbing child very roughly by the cheeks, clearly trying to quieten him. I gestured that he should not hurt the boy. At this time, Raju sensed my involvement, and came to tell me that the boy wanted to get back on the bus with his family instead of going to school, something we often experienced at school drop-off times with Gus. While I was uncomfortable about the physical nature of the interaction, who was I to get involved? I walked away with mixed feelings about the incident. As the child's family drove up the road the boy ran screaming after them, losing a sandal as he went. I grabbed it for him. The back half was worn down to nothing and one of the rubber straps had broken. I handed it to him as he walked back – having lost the fight to get back on the bus – and headed to school, tears still streaming down his face.

Aside from that event the day was very much a walk day. We had little interaction and few interesting experiences, and just put our head down and walked the twenty-six kilometres in around four-and-a-half hours – pretty good going. Nicola did an amazing job with her sore knee, and kept up for around fifteen kilometres, and then Bec, Nick and I finished the walk into Bidadi along the highway. The terrain was pretty uninspiring, uncomfortable and difficult. For most of the journey the dusty verge was a combination of crushed rocks – many the size of tennis balls. The only alternative was to walk on the edge of the road and trust that the speeding buses coming up from behind would have the courtesy to miss you. We chose to walk on the verge and every step was a challenge.

That night was our farewell dinner for Nicola and Eibhlin, who would be heading home the next day. We decided to have a pre-dinner drink at the leisure bar. Once again, in its day it would have been a thriving little hotspot. Unfortunately, it continued the theme of a ghost resort, with dusty glasses on the shelves behind the bar and a marked absence of water in the water feature. Regardless, we all had a great chat about our Indian adventure, and shared memories of Nicola and Eibhlin's time with us. Indy and Maggie dressed up and enjoyed their last night with the big girls. Meanwhile, Gus was on his scooter dodging bats and looking for bugs and spiders. He came up to me at one point and said he had a splinter. There was a little bit of blood on his finger, and it didn't seem serious. He then sheepishly let on that he had in fact cut his finger on a blade, which seems unthinkable really, but this is Gus we're talking about. He took me over to the water feature – basically an empty, small, tiled plunge pool. On its base there it was, a razor blade. I immediately grabbed Bec, and we had a mini meltdown thinking what could be on it, so I was sent down to retrieve the troublesome object. It was dark near the pool, and when I jumped over a bar onto some steps, they decided to give way. My foot went straight through and I grazed my shin. I awkwardly pulled myself out, climbed over the railing, and into the pool to retrieve the blade. Fortunately it was a new blade. There was no rust, blood, or any other visible problems.

Back in the room for some first aid, Gus very bravely and patiently waited as Bec doused him in every type of antiseptic she had available and taped up the little cut. In the scheme of Gus and his injuries this was very minor, and had we not been in India we probably wouldn't have done anything about it. Next, Bec turned her attention to my three bloody grazes, and took great pleasure in applying antiseptic. I wish I could say I was as brave as Gus but he was witness to his father's screams of agony as Bec worked her magic. Gus showed some Nurse Ratchet tendencies, as he tried to get involved and cause further pain. Fortunately that was the end of the drama for the evening. We returned to the abandoned restaurant and enjoyed our final dinner. This was not Bec's favourite place to stay, and in fact there was a general consensus that it was the worst accommodation we had encountered so far.

Day 16 Bidadi to Bangalore

On our sixteenth day, the walk team for the first leg included Nick, Nicola, Eibhlin and myself. We decided that Indy should take it easy, and Maggie was still asleep when we left. Poor Raju was just getting out of bed when we got to the car, so he quickly dressed and we were on the road, bellies full of homemade porridge, by 7.30 am. Once again, the morning's walk was quite straightforward. We were on the road to Bangalore, and with very few villages, we walked along the highway – the way growing more urbanised with each step. We stopped at a small roadside shop, and had the best coffee of the trip served in beautiful, clear glasses. Eibhlin gave Nick some last minute stretching advice as we waved to the school kids on the buses driving past. We heard word from the others that they had packed up and were on their way. Sure enough, a short time later the bus pulled up and we did the changeover. Eibhlin and Nicola said their goodbyes to Nick and myself, and Indy joined the walk team once again. We had walked around fifteen kilometres, and there were another twenty to Bangalore.

The three of us continued to walk as the girls and Gus headed to the hotel – or so we thought. As we progressed we hit the city fringe, and with it came smog, dust, traffic, and poor footpaths. Bangalore is known as the Garden City, and that's how I remembered it from our trip in 1996. Now it far more resembled the Concrete City, with a monorail under construction, and roads being built and reconstructed everywhere we looked. It was not an enjoyable walk into the city. We heard from the girls that they were caught in a gridlock traffic jam, and were going nowhere. The plan was to check into the hotel, for Nicola and Eibhlin to have a wash after their walk, and then head to the airport. Now the plan was to just try and get the girls to the airport in time for their flight. We also realised that Raju would not be back to collect us for several hours, so after a quick drink stop, we pressed on to find a spot in the city for a break. Again we found our way into a labyrinth of construction zones and traffic gridlock, and as pedestrians, we were not high on the priority list. A friendly police officer helped us cross one road, but after about fifteen minutes of very cramped and dusty traffic, I suggested we jump in an auto and head into the city. Nick had a better idea to head straight to the hotel.

We found ourselves a brand new auto and a driver who spoke English well. He agreed to take us to the hotel, using the tariff meter, which was not our usual experience but a welcome option. We were all very pleased to be out of the dust. Even the driver joked the garden city was more like a concrete city. He took great pleasure in pointing out the major attractions en route as we darted effectively through the traffic. The drive took over an hour, as our hotel was out of the city near the international airport. It appeared suddenly like an oasis as we drove along a dusty road. Pulling through the gate, we immediately entered another world of green grass, coconut trees, and an expansive garden. We were very relieved to see Raju, meaning the rest of the team had also arrived.

We had made it through six consecutive walk days, traversed almost 150 kilometres, and made it to our

Christmas rest stop. Here we would recharge, give the kids a chance to have a swim and rest their bodies and minds, and share Christmas together. My sister Kate and her kids – twelve-year-old Ally and nine-year-old Max – would be arriving soon, and we were all very excited. The kids were planning a special welcome ceremony at the airport with flower garlands and signs. We heard from Nicola and Eibhlin that they made good use of the butt washer at the airport to clean what they could, and were enjoying a relaxing drink as they waited for their plane. For the first time on the trip we had a two-bedroom apartment. The girls, of course, chose the master bedroom, and were busy organising their gear in the walk-in wardrobe. Bec and I were relegated to the loft bedroom, which we were not unhappy about.

The kids ordered up some fries and we all took a breath and relaxed. Jen and Nick were right next door, and we knew we were in for a nice stay.

Day 17 Rest Day

As you can imagine, we all looked forward to a sleep-in, enjoying the comfortable beds, clean sheets, and soft pillows. Considering our last stop where we slept in sleeping bags due to a fear of bed bugs, and the mattresses felt like hay on concrete, we were all grateful for a little bit of comfort. After breakfast we split up. Mum, Nick and Indy headed out with Raju to do a little shopping, and Bec, Maggie, Gus and I headed to the pool to relax.

It was a lovely and well-earned rest. The only moment of concern was when Gus bent over by the side of the pool complaining of a stomach-ache and cramps. Fortunately they passed quickly, and he was soon scooting around the hotel at a hundred miles an hour. You can't hold Gus down for long. Maggie enjoyed her fries by the pool, and while it was a little cool – only mid twenties – nothing could stop her from swimming if she got the chance, especially given it was the first clean pool we had found in India.

We had a lovely, quiet day. We reflected on the joy of a very different build-up to Christmas, without the usual stress and pressure. We planned to visit a children's orphanage and share gifts with them. It was the type of Christmas I had been dreaming of and I was very excited. We then planned to return to our hotel for a family Christmas dinner. Bec found a small tree branch, and decorated it with Mum and the kids. Our friends at the hotel went out of their way to make us feel at home by setting up a few Christmas decorations in our room.

We heard from Kate that they were ready to go, and by the time we woke up the next morning they would be on their way to join us.

Family Reunion

It was the evening of 23 December. We all stayed up late and had a dinner in the restaurant – something quite unique and exciting when travelling with a three-year-old. The girls got dressed up in their Indian finery – Indy in her Indian dress and Maggie in her sari. They looked very beautiful. Gus was in fine form, and kept not only us but also the waiting staff entertained. Nick wasn't feeling a hundred per cent so he decided to stick with the chicken soup, while the rest of us continued to eat our way across India with another lovely meal. We then packed into the Tempo Traveller with Raju and headed to the airport for a 10 pm pick-up. Given it was an international flight we had no idea if they would be on time. We were very pleased to see they arrived when expected, and we took our place outside the doors with other families and drivers. We stood there for nearly an hour, waiting for the plane to land, and for the clan to clear immigration and get their bags. Of course it seemed like an eternity to the kids as they watched each person come through the doors. Eventually we saw Kate's unmistakable golden curls, closely followed by Ally and Max. There were squeals of excitement all round and lots of hugs and kisses. As you can imagine it was very hard to get a word in with five very excited kids, and, come to mention it, five very excited adults.

On the drive home Maxy was very enthusiastic about the cows on the road; an excitement we weren't sure would last long. We were so happy to have him and Ally join in on our Indian adventure. We are very close and I love them like my own kids, as Kate does with ours. Ally has a touch of drama about her, often taking centre stage at family gatherings, which is interesting given she can be quite introverted at other times. Like her Mum, Ally often brings joy and laughter, and we can always rely on her to get the family singing. Maxy is quite similar to what I imagine I was like growing up. Born with a football in his hands, he loves his sport and is a very talented athlete at whatever he turns his hands to. He is also a quiet and sensitive young kid who sometimes struggles to find the words to express himself. He has a great interest in why things happen, especially between people. All of the kids, especially the oldest four, have a very special bond, and our family has a lot of energy when we are all together.

Christmas in Bangalore

We started celebrating on Christmas Eve with a lovely family dinner on a couple of trestle tables that we had brought into our room, a read of 'The Night Before Christmas' – a family tradition – and then an early night. Maggie left out a few snacks for Santa and the reindeers with the hope they would find their way to Bangalore. The tooth fairy had found us, so surely Santa would too.

I slept in one bedroom with Gus, and Bec slept in the other with the girls. Gus was particularly excited about leaving a pillowcase by the end of the bed, and Santa coming to fill it during the night. I awoke on Christmas morning to Ally and Max's footsteps in the next room – they were still on Adelaide time. After a short time Gus started to stir, and I quietly reminded him about his sack at the end of the bed. He jumped up like I'd given him a shot of adrenaline, and, still bleary-eyed, found his presents. We grabbed the sack and headed down to the girls' room to wake them.

Gus opened his presents first, followed by Maggie and Indy. It was a pretty modest set that year, but we enjoyed them just as much as usual. We opened up the doors and wished a happy Christmas to Jen, Nick, Kate and the kids. After breakfast we packed up and headed out to the Sneha Care Home and Shining Star School for children infected with HIV. It was very strange driving through the streets of Bangalore, as only around five per cent of the population is Christian, so Christmas Day is not a big affair.

The drive took us over an hour, and we arrived to find large grounds containing a church, housing, farming area, vegetable garden, and most importantly the school itself. We arrived a little early and, as the children were still at their morning mass, we had a short tour of the classrooms. They were full of colour and information designed to create a positive learning environment. There were approximately a hundred orphaned children aged four to twelve who lived at the home and attended the school. They were able to receive the medical attention they required, as well as a nutritious diet that enabled healthier kids. We were later informed that the life expectancy for many of these children if left in their villages was only thirteen or fourteen years of age. The staff went to great lengths to identify living relatives, and help the children retain links with them.

After a while, small groups started to make their way back from the church to the classrooms. We were very excited to see them. Courtesy of ChildFund India and the funds we had raised we were able to, in discussion with the school, identify a range of sports equipment and games that the children would enjoy. Of course we had cricket sets, as well as badminton, board games, frisbees, skipping ropes and carrom boards – a kind of Indian finger snooker. It was a very informal visit and we basically just spent a few hours playing with the kids. Someone started singing Christmas songs, and soon we all joined in. Bec's bubbles again proved to be a hit, and had many children in raptures. Gus was playing and running with a large group of kids, while others were sitting and talking. I took a moment to stand there and take in what was happening around me. Usually by that stage on Christmas Day we would be on to our third or fourth drink, eating more than any person should consume in one day, and sharing a multitude of gifts. There isn't anything wrong with this, and in fact we were back to doing it the next year. That year was different though. It was an amazing day, and one to be remembered.

We finished our tour of the classrooms, and were then shown the dormitories, kitchen and offices. Father Matthew, who was the chaplain and essentially head of the school, discussed his plans and the land he had available for a vocational training centre for the children, so when they finished school there would be an option for them to continue their education and be trained in skills that would lead to employment. The centre received funding from the United States Agency for International Development, or USAID, for many years, and the year we visited marked the end of that funding. Father Matthew was quite positive about it, and said he was confident funds would come in from somewhere. I certainly hoped so. This was one of the most important services I could imagine for children who were desperately in need of nourishment, medication, love and support. We discussed other needs for the children and Father Matthew expressed his interest in making spirulina available, particularly for their most malnourished children. Two children had already started the treatment, and he was interested in increasing this number. (A check later was reassuring. As of 2014, the school was receiving local, foreign and corporate funding to assist with vocational support, purchase library books and computers, and pay for medical treatment at a local hospital.)

Our kids had a look at where the children lived. It was clean and well organised, and looked like a camp centre that many children enjoy during school trips. The reality, however, was that it was daily life. There were two rooms for the boys and two rooms for the girls. Each child had one bunk bed, and one locker in a room shared with twenty or thirty others. In recent trips, these were the kinds of encounters that stayed with our kids, so I was happy that Ally and Max got to share in the experience.

We spent some time saying our goodbyes before the children went to lunch. We headed back to the hotel and took a moment to absorb all that our morning had meant to us. We returned to our rooms, shared some small gifts, and then enjoyed our dinner together. It was a very special Christmas Day, and we hoped that our friends and family also shared a very happy day of their own.

Day 22 Visit to ChildFund India in Bangalore

It was our last morning at the Angsana, a luxurious hotel, but as each day went by, we – at least the adults – enjoyed the comfort less and less. We longed to be back on the road doing what we came here for. Day twenty-two was a welcome change as we were heading to the

ChildFund India national office in the centre of Bangalore.

The drive was shorter than we expected, and we arrived about half an hour early. We were greeted by our good friends Prem Kumar and Antony, and had an opportunity to meet Esther, Peter and many other staff. Shortly after our arrival a carload of ChildFund sponsored children arrived to join our walk. A couple of the staff also brought their daughters, aged six and eight, so Gus was in his element with two young ladies to entertain. Fortunately a large wall surrounded the ChildFund office, so they could run wild without any danger.

We enjoyed some tea and snacks with the staff and children, and they told us about the sponsors. One child's sponsor was from Sweden, another was from Denmark, and another was the Murphy family in Australia. These kids are living proof of the value a monthly commitment makes. It was something we had already seen many times on our journey.

The press were due to arrive between 10 am and 11.30 am for a couple of interviews, and they started to show up close to 11.30 am when we were hoping to start our symbolic walk around Bangalore. A few quick photos were taken, and we had an interview with a journalist. Nick, Indy, Bec and I contributed our thoughts on the walk so far. The children had been waiting downstairs to commence our walk with placards, banners, and buckets to collect more funds. We were soon able to make our way across the road to a Toyota car showroom, and as the kids went in two more journalists arrived.

Both Gus and Indy were tired, so I took them back to the office and within a few minutes Gus was asleep. Indy also felt better for the rest. Maggie, Ally and Max continued on with the rest of the team. We shortened the fundraising walk as we had a few other things to do, so within ninety minutes the team had returned to the office with many rupees in their buckets, and sat down to a wonderful Indian lunch. Gus was still fast asleep on my lap and Indy's, but Indy managed to wriggle out, later commenting it was the best meal she had eaten in India. There was a mild butter chicken and some tandoori chicken, as well as a beautiful chickpea and beetroot curry. She came running down at one stage for a drink, complaining that the food was too spicy, but that she loved it so much she couldn't stop eating it. She also told me that she was in the middle of another interview – this time over the phone. We encouraged the kids to have free reign with the media and say whatever they wanted to. After all, this was their trip too.

After lunch we transported Gus to the vehicle and jumped in to visit two schools out on the rural fringe in the Kolar district. ChildFund staff had taken on the schools as personal projects, supporting them with their own efforts and funds. We drove up to a small school to find a sea of beautiful smiling faces, followed by a flurry of handshakes and greetings. We had tea and cookies with the staff and children, and visited the three school classrooms of children in years one to six. We also had the opportunity to visit the preschool kids and distribute spirulina candies. Antony shared with us that the community were in the middle of a spirulina trial, and recorded the weights and nutrition of each of the children. They were only weeks in, and there were already positive results emerging much to Antony's delight. The evidence of the support of the ChildFund staff was everywhere; water filters, books, toys, and desks among many other items. We saw the children's work, sang songs and had the pleasure of distributing books – again quite informally – before we reluctantly said goodbye.

We drove a short distance and arrived at our second school. By this stage it was 4.30 pm, and understandably the children were preparing to go home. Even though it was the end of the day they were very hospitable, and we had the joy of singing each of our national anthems before another cup of tea and a final cookie for the day. Our visit had identified the need for computers and desks, and we asked our ChildFund friends to supply us with further information regarding what else was required. As always, the visible dedication and enjoyment of the staff was inspiring. We took some time saying our goodbyes. Local families came from everywhere at these events, and there were always many people to talk to.

The spirit in the bus was very positive as we headed to our accommodation at the SN Resort. We chose a more rural setting, once again opting to drive out of Bangalore rather than walk through the urban construction zones. As we approached, Ally was quietly working herself into a frenzy of concern about the likely state of our accommodation, probably not helped by my occasional comments. We had no idea what was in store for us – other than the fact it was at the lower end of the cost scale at $20 per room, per night. As often happened on the trip I was pleasantly surprised by what we found. It was, of course, extremely basic. There were two single beds and a cold shower in each room, but it was quite clean and tidy. A bustling vegetarian restaurant downstairs was also a good sign, and after settling in, and organising a couple of extra mattresses, we had a nice meal and went to bed.

Day 23 Community Walk and Visit in Bangarapet

That morning was slow. We were exhausted after a long day, and had an early start with a pick up at 8 am. We planned to drive to a local town where we would walk with a group of people and visit many ChildFund projects. Before that, we had a quick stop at a large temple surrounded in showground-like stalls, which was quite surreal. Within the temple was another temple where a blessing took place. Gus found this entertaining for only so long, so I followed him outside. Bec later informed me that part of the ceremony was the opportunity to drink from the holy plate. Nurse Ratchet declined the offer. Mum – determined to make the most of every experience – took a drink, and sensing Bec's hesitation turned to her and with an assuring tone said, 'It's holy water, Bec.'

We arrived in Bangarapet to find a huge crowd waiting for us – the biggest on our journey so far. The local politician immediately greeted us, and we had flower garlands placed on our heads, blessings for team members, and, of course, photos. As we set off, sponsored children and hundreds of school kids accompanied us. You had to be there to truly understand how amazing it was. There was a line up of people following us for hundreds of metres. I turned to Kate, still getting acclimatised on her first trip to India and told her to just go with it. We walked through the main street of the local town, and after a short time, the school kids said their goodbyes and headed back to school. Gus was on my shoulders, and I was careful to give him a little more comfort than in previous crowds. Ally and Maxy were having their first walking experience and I couldn't imagine what must have been going through their minds. A week ago they were in Adelaide, and there they were, walking across India with their family and surrounded by hundreds of other people. Ally maintained a confident stride, while Maxy struggled to hide his amazement with his widening brown eyes.

We soon came across a small gathering of children and teachers waiting for our arrival. We stopped for a greeting, another blessing, some cookies (clearly an Indian favourite), and an impromptu dance presentation. After half an hour we continued on to a primary school. There was an entrance party like a guard of honour and marigold petals flying around us. We spent some time in the classroom with the teachers and kids, shared a few words, and of course saw some dancing. While there, the principal of this small school introduced us to one of his students, Nicholaas, who had scored in the top four out of 1000 students in recent exams. As a result, he won a scholarship for the remainder of his education.

At that time there were two classrooms and a kitchen, and there were plans to build a dining hall. It was clear that the school put a great deal of care and dedication into their teaching. The walls and ceilings were covered in the children's work and teaching materials. The principal informed us that the school needed a computer, and they hoped this was something that could result from our visit. We were very happy when ChildFund informed us that this had been achieved.

The children from the school joined us for the next leg of the walk, the youngest slowly dropping off in age groups. We walked for some time, and stopped again at a local college. We could immediately see that although there were large grounds, there were no buildings other than an administrative office. A throng of older students greeted us as a man stood up to speak and asked Mr Donald to sing for us. Nothing happened, as he couldn't be found. Just when the crowd was starting to grow restless, he appeared out of nowhere, and stepped onto the veranda. He was a slight, young man, and when he opened his mouth he sang in a beautifully clear voice.

I was then asked to share a few words. It is always difficult to speak to a group where there is little context. We were unsure as to what we were doing there, or what the group wanted to know. The principal spoke next, and it became clear that they were asking for funding for their classrooms – a project well beyond our means. He explained how their college grew from forty to 220 students. One particularly touching comment was, 'Every tree is a classroom.'

We were nearing the end of our walk, and scheduled to visit one more school. Many kids were waiting for us, and again there were dances and speeches. I still got the impression that people thought we were crazy walking from coast to coast. We ensured this was only a quick visit, as we could smell the kids' lunch waiting for them, and Indian's take their mealtimes very seriously.

We then had for a short walk to Grama Vikas – the non-governmental organisation, or NGO, that managed the implementation of the ChildFund projects – and were invited to take a rest on the roof. There was some temporary scaffolding with large, heavy-duty material curtains to make an Arabian-like tent for us for lunch. We could see kids running around and waving to us behind the offices. There were also a family of monkeys running around, who provided great entertainment to our lot. We had a beautiful lunch of pumpkin, potato, eggplant, pappadums, chapatti, tomato soup, gulab jamun, and bananas. It was an absolute feast, and I was proud of the kids who all ate well. It didn't take long for the monkeys to cotton on to the smell, and every now and again one would poke their head out from behind the curtains looking for a snack. The staff would approach them with their 'monkey stick' and they would flee, but only for a short time before returning for another raid. There was a monkey sitting only a foot away, eyeing the food, then the kids, then the food. Eventually he was brave enough to launch an attack, grabbed a banana peel, and took off. Seconds later – clearly not happy with his haul – he returned, this time for a chapatti. Of course the kids found this to be great entertainment.

After lunch we were asked to move to the community hall, some fifty metres down the road. As we came around the corner, we were once again amazed to see a large crowd of children and adults amassed around an open-air community stage. It held dignitaries – perhaps twenty-five of them – large speakers, and a local politician seated on a long table. As we made our way up onto the stage and looked out we saw hundreds of smiling faces. When we greeted them with a 'hi', we received a uniform wave, a smile, and a group 'hi' in return. There was no limit to the number of times this could happen, and as you can imagine, Gus in particular enjoyed the game.

The event started with speeches from the Grama Vikas staff and managers. I was asked to speak once again, and was followed by the local politician. Fortunately the speeches didn't last too long, and it was over to the performers. We all quickly jumped off the stage to get a front row seat with the kids. Nick and Bec took vantage points for some camera work, while I sat with Gus on the floor with a few children. Almost immediately I felt this little arm link in with mine, and looked next to me to see a beautiful, smiling face of a young boy named Akram. Quite naturally he leaned in for a cuddle, and together we watched and enjoyed the show. Prem later told me that the whole ceremony was the idea of the children and staff, who had complete control over how the event unfolded. It was also a dress rehearsal for the kids who would perform at the ChildFund India sixtieth birthday colobrations in Delhi. There was no doubt that this would be a highlight. It would rival any opening ceremony of the Olympics. The stage was full of performers in colourful outfits – some traditional, others adorned in peacock feathers. It was a blast of colour and sound.

After the performances we distributed twenty bikes to schoolgirls and twenty-seven water filters for schools – it was our favourite part of the day. Ally and Max got to experience the honour of giving them to their recipients, which I thought was especially important given that only a few weeks ago they had been raising funds for these very items.

We then took the opportunity to meet many of the children and performers and thank them for their wonderful efforts. Gus was always a popular target, although he had almost perfected saying, 'No, no, no. No hugging, no cheek pinching,' with a slight Indian accent. We made sure one of us was with him at all times. We walked back to the office and on the way met a young girl who had been given one of the new bikes. With Prem as my interpreter, I asked her what difference it would make to her life. She said that each day she was required to travel fifteen kilometres to attend college, and the cost of the auto was too high. It turned out that she was Akram's sister, and a sponsored child from a nearby village. Akram of course came along for his fifth goodbye, and we enjoyed a coffee with some of the staff. Maxy tried his first cup and was hooked. He was already a bundle of energy, so we weren't sure what would happen with a caffeine hit. Fortunately Indian coffee is very milky and weak.

It was a very long day. Despite feeling a little tired at lunchtime, the kids seemed to fully grasp the meaning of the day, and were almost hyper on our drive back to the hotel. There were all the famous family songs: 'Glenelg Spelt Backward is Glenelg', 'Tintinara Kicks Forward', 'The Wombat Song', 'Barry Evil Song', 'I Want to Be Like Poppa'. All, of course, made up by Poppa, and now a family tradition to sing with great joy and at great volume. Poor Raju got to experience it firsthand.

Day 24

Bangarapet to Bethamangala

That morning we had a slightly later start, yet were still ready to leave at 8.30 am. After a couple of days with small walks, we were very excited about the prospect of getting back on the road and punching out a full twenty kilometres. It was the first full day of walking for Kate, Max and Ally, and Nick, Indy, Maggie and I joined them. We decided to drive to Bethamangala, and then walk back to Bangarapet where we were staying. The kids looked great and were ready for the day. Mum, Bec and Gussy had a short shopping list, and stayed in the car with Raju. Gus was excited at the prospect of getting a battery for the plane he was given for Christmas.

We set off, and as often happened, the first couple of hours were the most difficult for the new walkers. Ally in particular was struggling to get into her stride, but maintained her pace well with the group. After a short time we came across the very impressive New Oxford School. As we walked past the front gates we could see a presentation, and a teacher quickly spotted us and invited us onto the stage. I'm not really sure why, but how can you refuse when asked? There were hundreds of kids, and a few very official gentlemen sat on the stage and gave speeches. Some extra chairs were supplied and up we went. We thought were going to have a quiet walking day. We were wrong. We were again presented with beautiful flower garlands, although this time we were spared the need to make a speech. The event was an exhibition of the students' work for the term. Many of those seated in the courtyard had brought produce, nuts, and toys with them and had made their own market. Kate enquired how long we would be there, and I again said, 'No idea. Let's just go with it.'

Fortunately the speeches were short, and we were able to follow the other dignitaries around the student markets. Afterwards we headed up to the classrooms to view exhibitions of the students' work. It was of an incredibly high standard. They had each been given a topic such as deforestation, traditional music, volcanoes and zoos, and made large displays accompanied by both written and verbal presentations of their work. They then presented their exercise books for feedback and signature. Maggie in particular thought that giving out her autograph was pretty cool. We could have easily spent all day there, and found it hard to break away given we were continually encouraged to see just one more presentation. Eventually we left, and even then managed to disappoint a number of students.

We had to continue on. Indy led, followed by Maggie and Maxy, who were either singing at high volume or talking non-stop. All the kids seemed happiest when we were chatting and telling stories. We shared old stories of our dogs and cats and the troubles they got themselves into for many kilometres. There wasn't too much time to stop and enjoy the scenery because when we weren't telling stories there were requests for drinks, food and other general grievances. It was quite an effort to keep everyone motivated, fed, watered, and walking.

We had a stop around a third of the way for soft drinks, chips and chocolate, which seemed to give the kids a boost of energy. We set course for the bakery we saw on the way that morning, and it seemed to keep them focus. They were doing an amazing job and Kate, Poppa and I moved between them to keep them going. There was the occasional complaint about sore feet, or the expected, 'How long till we get there?' but overall they were brilliant. Before we knew it we made it to the bakery where we had soft drinks, pineapple juice, and an assortment of sweet treats for the kids. We knew we had broken the back of the walk, and it was only a matter of a few kilometres back to the hotel through a very busy Bangarapet township. A quick guessing game of what time we would make it back, and the kids were kept focused until the end. Forty-five minutes and three kilometres later we made it. It was a solid twenty kilometres in total and with five kids in tow we had done well. Nick had a sore hip and retired to do some stretches while Bec and mum shared stories of their day, and that they were once again organised after a busy week. The kids were clearly pretty happy with themselves and retired for a rest and a couple of movies. We had a shower, ordered up some coffees, and we watched a slideshow of Bec's photos.

Bec and I were now twenty-four days into our family adventure. Each day was beautiful, inspiring, challenging, difficult, and every other adjective you can come up with. Sometimes just getting the kids ready in the morning seemed like an unachievable target, at other times the most challenging tasks appeared easy and comfortable. I don't think that completing this walk as adults would be particularly difficult, but travelling with three families and five young kids was testing at times, as I am sure you can imagine. Our kids were doing incredibly well given it was the longest we had ever travelled overseas, and we were into uncharted territory. Indy and Mags were particularly enjoying having their nanna, poppa, aunty and cousins with them. Gus had been an absolute champion, even after days of nine hours of activities and walking. Given we had been travelling overseas since he was four months old, and the three kids had been to East Timor, Thailand and on multiple trips to India, they were well conditioned for this trip. Bec continued to be amazing, an absolute powerhouse. She got everyone organised, cared for Gus, supplied nursing services to all, provided amateur photography, was a counsellor for anyone in need, and a wonderful role model to our children.

Day 25

Bethamangala to Venkatagirikota: into the eye of the cyclone

As we retired on day twenty-four, we noticed a few rain clouds gathering. Since we had arrived in India, the mornings had been clear and cool, with warm or hot afternoons and cooler evenings. Each day was beautiful, clear, and sunny. Not for day twenty-five!

The winds were very strong during the night. It was

raining that morning when we awoke, and by the state of the car park, it seemed to have been happening for some time. It was our first wet day, and on only day two for Kate and the kids. Bec and I had halved our luggage at our last stop from four backpacks to two to limit the gear we had to take into each hotel. Of course the wet weather gear was in the other backpack in the car with Raju. Mum agreed to have Gus today, and Ally decided she wanted a rest day as she was feeling a little tired, so the walk team consisted of Indy, Mags, Maxy, Poppa, Kate, Bec, and me. We planned to walk around eighteen kilometres.

We drove to the spot where we had started our walk the day before. A little confusing for all involved but logistically it ended up being the way to go. The drive revealed that it had indeed been raining for some time, as the dry, dusty roads we were used to had turned to mud. The anxiety levels in the bus were slightly heightened as we tried to comprehend the day ahead. Kate gently reminded us that in her last email she asked if she needed wet-weather gear, to which we responded, 'Nah, she'll be right.' Famous last words. Between us we had four spray jackets: Nick and Indy had theirs, and Bec and I gave our recently retrieved jackets to Maggie and Max.

We stepped out of the bus into strong, slanting rain. As we headed off down the road, Maggie turned to me and asked, 'Do you think people think we are crazy?' I told her I thought so, and that sometimes I agreed with them. A few steps later, and I asked if she would prefer to be at Lakes Entrance with our friends the Buckleys, sitting in her uncle Paul's leather recliner eating her favourite chips, or walking in the rain in India. This sent her into a spin.

She spent several kilometres chastising me for the fact that she was missing out on her favourite Christmas holiday with our good friends to walk along a rural road in India in the rain and mud. Maggie was vocal in her views – and a little physical – but it was all in good fun.

I commented to the team that it looked like it was clearing up – something I would repeat often during the day. In reality, all we could see ahead was a big, grey cloud. The group made up a song about crazy Aussies walking in the rain, and despite the conditions everyone remained in good spirits. Our shoes and clothes were wet through within minutes. It would be a long day. Maggie was once again singing, joined by Maxy for a barber's duet. Bec and Kate, aka Prude and Trude, were chatting away, and Nick and Indy were walking together. Nick, having felt unwell the night before with stomach pains, was showing no signs of discomfort, and was making good ground. As we walked along we received some very strange looks from the locals. Even the cows found shelter, and smirked as we walked past. One man on his motorcycle took pity on us, and offered us to spend some time under his hay shelter. We gratefully declined and pressed on.

The kids were getting a little preoccupied with their wet shoes and socks, and after letting it go for a while, I gathered them up and shared the story of Victor Frankyl. The moral of the story was that you cannot always control your environment, but Victor believed and in fact demonstrated that you can control your mind. It may have been a bit heavy for the crew but it seemed to do the trick. I also talked with Maxy about playing footy in the rain – which perhaps had more impact, and was easier for a nine-year-old to relate to.

We walked along for some time – the kids bouncing along the road with great energy. We found our way to a small town, a once dirt road turned to mud, and a few shops scattered along the way. Prude and Trude yelled out for a coffee stop, and I glanced right to see a galvanised shed with steaming coffee on the boil. We pulled up to a small shelter where a number of people were taking cover from the rain; looking quite bizarre I am sure. A couple of the men encouraged us to come in under the shelter, and made way to show a bench for us to sit at. We shuffled the kids in to take a seat and ordered up our coffee. The barista stood at the old cobbled wooden bench, gas grill plate on the go, with a small metal saucepan that he filled with a few scoops of milk taken from a metal bucket on the bench. He grabbed six small glasses, added a spoon of sugar, and then emptied a sachet of coffee between the glasses. By this time the milk had boiled, and he poured it into the cups. The next step was traditionally Indian, as he grabbed a small metal cup, poured in the coffee from one glass, and did a long pour from the cup back to the glass – a routine he repeated three or four times in order to cool it down. By that stage people were coming from everywhere to sit and watch these strange visitors having their morning coffee. And boy was that good coffee! So good we had to order seconds as we enjoyed a few minutes out of the rain.

I made some small talk with a group of young men in the shelter. After the usual, 'Which Country' conversation, we spoke the international language of cricket. I reminded the boys that Australia had just gone one nil up in the test series, to which I may have struck a nerve. We then went through a range of cricketers' names. I said Ponting, they said batsman. I said Warne, they said bowler, and so on. The kids huddled together under the shelter, enjoying their drinks. Kate sat next to them with a smile from ear to ear as she experienced her first genuine Indian coffee. A crowd of over fifty people – mostly boys and men – were gathering to observe. We were clearly the best show in town on a drizzly Indian morning.

With health and energy levels restored, the team was off and running. We grabbed extra supplies at the next shop and Kate bought a few chocolate bars for the local kids standing by. We found a spot between two small buildings and huddled around to help an uncomfortable Maggie change out of her wet T-shirt, although it had not stopped raining, which made her feel better even if only for a short time. Every stop involved many smiles and hellos, with a few words shared, and we always managed to draw a crowd. Off we went again up the road and into the rain, shoes sloshing full of water. The spirit among the team was remarkably high for the conditions as we made our way through the mud and the puddles and the rain. At one point a small van pulled over and asked if we needed a ride, to which Maggie and Maxy smiled in anticipation. We declined the offer, much to their disappointment. The road we were walking along was more rural than we were used to, and so we were not as confident about the direction we were taking. At one point we stopped at a small bus shelter and found a couple of young boys on a motorbike, and we took the opportunity to ask for directions. Fortunately we were heading in the right direction. We pressed on.

The rain was relentless, so we decided to 'call in the air support' and phone Raju, thinking it would take him an hour or so to get to us. Sure enough, around ten minutes later, Raju appeared. Maggie tried to convince Maxy to get on board, but as he wanted to finish the walk, Maggie also stayed with us. Kate and Bec decided they needed to test out the 'bush toilet' after all the coffee they had consumed. They waited for Raju to head up the road and found a friendly bush to squat behind. They returned to the team happier for the relief, and managed to avoid the snakes and thorns. As we walked past a concerned Raju and the parked bus further up the road, I mentioned to him that it was very wet, to which he replied, 'Yes Sir, it is the Madras Cyclone.' So that explained the poor weather. Nick recalled seeing something on the Indian news that looked like large waves crashing into the shoreline somewhere, we just didn't know where. We didn't have internet access so we were pretty much flying blind. Given the weather of recent weeks the last thing we would have thought of was a cyclone. Only in India and only on the coast to coast adventure!

On this final leg we crossed the border into our third Indian state. We had started our trip in Kerala, walked through Karnataka, and then made our way into the bottom end of the state of Andhra Pradesh. It would be a short visit, as we would soon be making our way to our final state of Tamil Nadu. We walked the final eight kilometres of the day, making good pace and walking around six kilometres an hour – some of the fastest waking we had done so far.

Maggie was fine as long as you kept her talking. She was very fit and could have probably walked fifty kilometres in a day. Max too was very fit, and managed to do the walk comfortably. We took our photo in front of the 'Welcome to' billboard, and our walk day was finished – over eighteen kilometres in the pelting rain and wind of the edge of a cyclone!

It was a great day by the team – the kids especially were incredible. News from Raju suggested that we may have up to seven days of rain ahead, and although we departed from our new accommodation the day after, we were still yet to receive confirmation of our next stay. We planned to head to RUHSA (Rural Unit for Health and Social Affairs) where Bec and I came as students in 1996. The accommodation and food would be the most basic of the trip, yet it was the stop I was most looking forward to. Bec and I shared many special memories there, and it would be great to share these with the rest of the family.

Twenty-six days on the road Life is hard

Travelling through rural India with a young family can be hard work. There was very little quiet time. Gus was in need of constant attention, and we often had to provide it in small hotel rooms. The older kids required support, as well as attention. They were often hungry, needed help finding their clothes, and wanted to spend time with us.

Bec and I sometimes went days without much more than a quick cuddle and kiss goodnight. We hadn't actually slept in the same bed more than a few times on the trip. For the majority of the trip, Gus had slept with one of us in a single bed, one of the girls slept in the other bed, and the other two would sleep on a small mattress on the floor – it was far from luxury.

We had cold showers most of the time, which wasn't great given it was quite cool in the mornings and evenings. Gus's hair resembled a Steelo pad, with a matt of shoulder-length blond tangles, which, I was sure, would be dreadlocks by the end of the trip. Maggie quite liked avoiding showering. She claimed that walking through the rain the day before was her wash. Indy liked to be clean and organised, so the lack of warm water troubled her somewhat more.

Each day someone was in pain – usually it was a stomach cramp that varied in severity. Fortunately it had only been a bit of wind so far. Nick's health was gradually deteriorating, although you wouldn't know it with his 'soldier on' mentality. He had not been eating or drinking, as it made him feel sick, and despite our encouragement of medication and a rest day, he was determined to work his way through whatever he was suffering from. It was nothing serious but remained a concern to the rest of the team.

I was trying to capture as much of our journey as possible. It usually involved me typing very quickly at the end of the day while I tried to shut out the noise of the kids running around and the rest of the adults debriefing.

The place we had stayed in for the four previous nights

was slightly mysterious. Loud banging came from the front of the hotel at strange hours of the night. The light in our room would come on at around 4 am – much to Indy's disgust. By the end of our stay the washing had piled in a small mountain, and we had clothes hanging from every possible spot. The hotel management told us off for having clothes hanging out the window. They did have standards; we just struggled to work out what they were.

We hadn't had internet access for the previous five days, and were feeling closed off from the rest of the world. Given that this meant we hadn't been able to secure our next accommodation stop, we hoped first of all that we could find RUHSA, second that they were expecting us, and third that the available accommodation would be enough for us all. After all, it was a rural hospital and development centre, not a hotel.

Fortunately each day there were far more special moments. The afternoon coffee debrief was always a highlight, and simply interacting with the people we met and our environment made everything worthwhile. Life on the road was hard, but it was what we signed up for. We were tested every day in every possible way, but everyone on the team stepped up, dug deep, and brought their A-game. We were working hard as a family to face all of the impending challenges, and were managing to keep our heads above water.

We heard that the cyclone in Chennai had already claimed over thirty lives, and when you saw the living conditions in India, you could easily imagine how this was possible. It was sobering news, and we took a minute to think about the people – and in particular the children – living on the street who are sick and vulnerable to the elements. What would happen to them? Where would they go for shelter, warmth, and safety? I didn't know, and found it hard to think about what would be in store.

Our troubles were tiny and temporary compared to those we saw on our travels. We went on our journey for an enhanced perspective, for a challenge, and to achieve our Big Hairy Audacious Goal – so far the adventure had provided all of this and more. I often reflected on a passage from M. Scott Peck's book *The Road Less Travelled*, where he writes, 'Life is difficult'. He continues, 'This is a great truth, one of the greatest truths'.

He suggests the challenge is that many people seek out a life that is easy, because it's the life everybody else supposedly has, which he asserts 'of course isn't the case'. He says: 'Life is a series of problems. Do we want to moan about them or solve them? Do we want to teach our children to solve them?' He suggests that once we accept that life is difficult then life is no longer seen as difficult, and the pain of solving problems can be accepted as part of life.

We reminded ourselves that this was why we were in India.

Meanwhile, Gus was kicking at the door wanting to go to the park downstairs closed due to the relentless rain. He had been stuck inside for forty-eight hours and had a healthy dose of cabin fever as a result. Not the ideal scenario for a three-year-old boy who loves to run and play. It was one of the more challenging times on the walk for Gus.

Day 26
Venkatagirikota to Pernampattu

We planned to walk from where we finished the day before on to Pernampattu. Raju would drop us off, and then take Bec, Mum, and Gus to the next accommodation spot. The first thing we noticed was that Raju set off in a different direction from the one we took the day before. At first we assumed it was just a quicker route along the highway. After asking Raju, we realised we needed a permit; without it we would face a large fine. The permit office was, of course, quite far from where we were starting the day. The drive had been a little hairy in patches, with lots of traffic on roads barely bigger than one lane. We had also been in the car for over an hour, and the kids were starting with, 'I feel sick', and, 'How long until we get there?'

After a quick consultation of the map, I made the call to drive straight to our accommodation, and then consider walk options from there. The RUHSA was a place of mixed memories for Bec and me. On one hand it was full of wonderful doctors and development workers, and on the other it was one of the most bureaucratic places I had visited, so I wasn't sure if our stay would be within the rules. I wanted to be there for check-in as I expected there to be problems. I wasn't disappointed.

The RUHSA was in a small town called K.V. Kuppam, around fifteen kilometres east of Gudiyatham. We didn't have the address, so I was working from memory. This worried Raju, but after several assurances that I knew what I was doing he drove on – worried frown still in tow. I knew we were getting close, and soon enough Bec spotted a sign and yelled, 'RUHSA!' We had made it. By this stage, both Max and Gus were dying to go to the toilet, and the rest of the team were keen to escape having driven through a fairly windy and rough section of road to get here. I walked into the office – memories flooding back with every step. I was pleased to locate Vinoth, who I had emailed regarding accommodation, and even more pleased that he was expecting us. In true RUHSA style, I was asked to sit as he looked for some time at his computer. He then pointed out the accommodation options, which consisted of two apartments and a double room that suited us pretty well given the circumstances.

Another staff member, who I remembered from my previous visits, escorted us to view the accommodation. Previously, I stayed in a very small room, with two basic single beds, and a small bathroom with a toilet, a cold shower, and a basin that drained out onto the concrete floor. It was pretty hard going for the three-month stay, but this time I was looking forward to the simplicity of it and felt prepared for our stay. We were initially escorted to view the two apartments. They were much larger than the old rooms, with a bedroom, living area, bathroom (with hot water), fridge and even a simple kitchen with a concrete bench and burner. It was much more comfortable than last time.

We then followed our escort to the double room intended for Jen and Nick, which could not have been further away. Jen whispered, 'Gee, we will need bikes to come and see you guys.' I know my mum well enough to know that was code for 'I don't like that we are being separated'. While the room was quite nice, it was not going to work for us. I headed back to the office, filled out a request for a room, and waited to speak with the director. In the meantime, the request book could not be found, and the staff members looked at each other asking where it was. I was called in to meet Dr Rita, the director at RUHSA, who was lovely and welcoming. As per RUHSA procedures, we had a discussion about my plans for the time I was there, and I assured Dr Rita it was purely a social visit, with no expectations on the staff.

We then met with the receptionist to discuss accommodation types. I asked if we could all stay together. The best I could arrange was to bring in additional beds, so we ended up with eight single beds for the ten of us. I could see that Mum was relieved with the outcome, and we were all happier having the team together.

We decided to settle in for the day given it was nearing 2.30 pm. Walking around the campus I ran into Mr Stalin, an old friend. I think he remembered me too, although he was calling me Patrick. One of the main reasons we wanted to return to RUHSA was to visit a family who lived nearby to the campus. They ran the K Paul Hotel nearby, named after the father of the family. It used to be a galvanised iron shed, but had grown to a concrete, open-walled establishment. The family was made up of Paul and Ama, and their five children. Both Bec and I had memories of being there in 1996, with Paul standing at the bench with his lungi and dirty white singlet overseeing operations. Then, Subashini was only a young girl with plaits, and

Christopher was a toddler running around saying, 'Hi.' We had kept in touch with Subashini and contributed to her education as we could. She was now a grown woman, married, and graduated as a nurse. She had caught a bus from a town some twenty-five kilometres away to see us again. Christopher had completed his Bachelor of Science, was about to start his Masters, and wanted to become a lecturer after completing his PhD. Roubia, their youngest daughter, was working with kindergarten-aged children at a nearby school. Paul was still standing at the bench with his lungi and white singlet.

Everyone was excited to see us and went to great lengths to offer us special meals. Despite our assurances that vegetarian food would be okay, they were determined to feed us chicken – I was able to curtail the offer of beef. Unfortunately, Nick and Maxy had been feeling unwell, and Mum kindly offered to stay with Gus who had fallen asleep just before we left. The rest of us joined the family for dinner in their house, and Subashini showed us her wedding DVD. We all sat together on the concrete floor in a small room of their small house. We shared two chicken curry dishes, and freshly cooked chapatti – one of my favourites. Their uncle from two houses up decided he would also cook us a special roast chicken dish, known as Chicken 65. We finally enjoyed a home-cooked, Indian meal, with one of our favourite Indian families. Indy and Maggie ate heartily, and we had a wonderful evening.

Day 27
K.V. Kuppam to Pernampattu

We awoke a little slowly but were still ready quite early. Unfortunately, poor little Maxy had his first encounter with Delhi Belly and was a definite no show. Kate stayed behind to look after him. Mum had the flu, and so became another member of the home team. Nick decided against advice from the team nurse, and despite having a tough night, set out for the day with Indy, Ally, Maggie and myself. Raju advised us that the road from Venkatagirikota was unsafe, so we instead decided to walk from RUHSA toward Pernampattu and see how far we could get. It unfortunately meant we were walking backwards, but it was the easiest way to go all things considered.

We walked for a few kilometres before Nick, Ally and Maggie decided to retire early, and caught an auto back to home base. Indy and I continued on up the road, determined to push out thirty kilometres. It was the first day just the two of us walked, and it was lovely to have the time together – with the usual stops for water and Lays chips along the way. We made it the first fifteen kilometres to Gudiyatham – a thriving, dusty, mini metropolis, with small, winding roads. We decided to press on, and though it was a difficult walk, we made it out the other end. We were trying to find tea bags but to no avail. Indy commented that India was organised chaos. She was right. Everything had a purpose and a way of happening, and everyone seemed to understand it but us.

On the other side of the town we experienced our first Indian altercation between one or two families. An older lady was pushing around an older man with a few cows, who was waving his stick and yelling a fair bit in return. Some younger women were also yelling at the man. In true Indian fashion, everyone still stopped and said hello as we walked past.

It was hotter than we had experienced since leaving Kerala, with temperatures pushing above thirty degrees. How we longed for the more temperate Bangalore climate. Indy and I commented that we better get used to it, as it would only grow hotter as we made our way to Chennai. We continued on and found that we were attracting the attention of the local dogs, who, for whatever reason, were more aggressive than others we had encountered – so much so that I grabbed a few rocks just in case. Indy felt unsafe, so after a very good effort, we decided to call it quits after twenty-five kilometres.

We rested up on a concrete bench next to the road in the middle of nowhere. The nearest major towns were ten kilometres in one direction and seven in the other. We sat and discussed our options – not that we had too many. Indy could see dogs in both directions so decided she wanted to stay put until an auto came along – the only other option being a bus. There wasn't much traffic so we sat and waited and chatted. Eventually a couple of autos passed by, but all with passengers on board. After a while, a man on a motorbike stopped to ask our name and what we were doing. He had some straw mats on his bike – one his way to or from a market. He took an interest in us and called over four or five of his friends, who were also on bikes with other items attached. They hailed down the next auto that came along, and negotiated initially on our behalf.

'How much to RUHSA?'

'330 rupees.'

'Tell him he's dreaming'; remembering of course that this was just over six dollars to travel twenty-five kilometres. I took over negotiation.

'How much to Gudiyatham?'

'150 rupees.'

'How about one hundred?' I got a shake of the head. I had clearly pushed too far, and my negotiation over one dollar cost us our ride. Our friends by this stage just looked at me and suggested the bus might be the best option – obviously for a cheapskate like me!

I asked our friends if where we were standing was a bus stop, knowing of course it wasn't, and they told me, 'No problem, bus will stop – number nine bus.' It came hurtling along only a couple of minutes later, and the men jumped into the middle of the road, pointing at the two Aussies pleading for it to stop. The whistle blew, and the bus pulled over. We jumped on board, thanking our friends for their troubles. What a generous offer to us as we sat there stranded. The system of ticket purchasing on the bus was very orderly – much to Indy's surprise – with a driver, ticket collector and conductor. It cost us twenty-two rupees to get back to RUHSA. We sat up the back and enjoyed Indy's first Indian bus experience. For a change, we were in the biggest vehicle on the road, and everyone got out of our way. A lady and her three children sat next to us, and we enjoyed a short conversation. As we approached the town of Gudiyatham, the ticket collector gestured to us about some food. I wasn't sure what he meant, but everyone was getting off the bus, so we followed suit and found shade under a verandah at the bus depot. A man came out with a spanner and went under the bus to do some quick repairs. I wasn't sure what good a spanner would be, but he seemed to know what he was doing.

While sitting at the depot, I noticed the young family sitting next to us had left their bag on the bus. I held onto it until the boy came back for it, gave it to him, and he thanked me and walked off. A few minutes later, he returned with a box of cake and offered us a piece each. As we continued to wait, the usual hawkers came around touting their wares – masala samosas, biscuits and sweets. You name it, they had it. Despite how good the samosas looked and smelled, we declined and eventually the bus took off back to RUHSA. Fifteen kilometres down the road, and people started gesturing to us that our stop was close – everyone taking good care of us. We jumped off and started walking, when a young man ran up and gave Indy back the hat she had left on the bus. It was another example of the kind and generous hospitality we received while there. I think sometimes people come to places like India and expect to get ripped off. We had the opposite experience. On four or five occasions we had shopkeepers run after us to return our change. We didn't have to barter for anything, except my effort with the auto, and everyone was extremely generous. It was a wonderful country with the most hospitable people.

After ninety minutes Indy and I finally arrived home, a little tired but very happy about our day and our time together. I had just enough time to enjoy a short sleep with Gussy before dinner. There was still no good news from next door, with many of the team feeling flat. Bec, our kids, Ally and I headed to Subashini's house for dinner. This time they had their bright pink nail polish out and were painting the girls' – and Gus's – nails on fingers and toes. They also arranged for henna tattoos, which were a big hit. Apparently our kids had asked for banana pancakes for dinner, which were sweet with lime and sugar, and made us realise how much we missed the food back home. Gus was kept entertained by the family as they played a multitude of games. It was another wonderful evening shared with our friends.

It was very special to watch how one family lived in such a small house, yet were so welcoming and hospitable. Friends and neighbours came and went, and Subashini's uncle came in every now and again with a new delicacy for us to try. He just wouldn't stop feeding us. We felt very close to their family, and very lucky to have the opportunity to be there together.

Day 28
Village walk around RUHSA

After a long walk the day before, and with many of the team slowly recovering, I suggested we walk through the local community around RUHSA. It was a very rural area with no large towns – mostly small enclaves of houses among farmland. They were the walks I enjoyed most from my previous visits to India. We all headed down to breakfast at the K Paul Hotel, and on the menu was fresh-made puri and, of course, beautiful coffee. Both Poppa and Maxy were ready to go after a tough twenty-four hours. Max was back to eating puri and potato curry – what a legend. Poppa eventually succumbed to Bec's pressure to take medicine, and he too had made almost a full recovery. He was back on the Indian diet, which was a big step given he had eaten nothing but plain rice for five days. We took turns watching Gus ride his scooter up and down the road, over bumps, and dodging the autos and motorbikes.

After breakfast as we headed out the gates of RUHSA, I saw a few faces I remembered, and spoke to a few friends. We made it a couple of hundred metres before hitting the train line, and saw a goods train blocking our way. We sat and waited like many others around us, as it was several hundred metres in each direction to go around. Our village walk was temporarily on hold. After a few comments from the kids that we had been waiting for hours, the train moved on – actually less than ten minutes from when we arrived. If I'm honest I was thinking about heading back and walking later. I am also not the most patient of individuals.

We walked along a newly bitumenised road that meant we were hot from the sun and the ground. Temperatures were topping over thirty degrees, and it was hotter earlier in the morning than we are used to. We walked along a road I ventured down in 2005, and I recalled all the photos I took, and the people I met. Most of the people remembered me more due to my old companion Frank, but either way was is was nice to revisit old friends. Gus was riding his scooter like a madman, and as usual attracted a lot of attention. We strolled through houses and farms for an hour or so, and with the day getting hotter, decided to return to the rooms for a rest. Bec, Kate and the kids arranged for a tour of the hospital at 1.30 pm, which Bec was looking forward to. In 1996 it was an amazing challenge for her, and she was keen to have a look to rekindle old memories. Gus and I chose to take an afternoon nap.

Later that afternoon, Bec and I took Gus up to the roof of the training hostel where we had stayed in 1996. Bec and I had spent so many nights up on the flat concrete roof looking up at the stars, often with our friend Frank, debriefing about our day – Bec in the hospital and me in the field. They were special memories, and I didn't realise how touching it would be for us to be back there together.

Gus had some more energy to burn – no surprises there – so I took him up to the road for another quick scoot. A few of the local kids, who we knew very well by that stage, ran with him up and down the road. He looked like he was leader of his own little gang. A monkey came by and had an interesting game of chasey with the local dogs, which was fun to watch. We then returned home to have a much-needed wash. The hot water service heated about a litre of water at a time, and came out of a tap. Once the hot water ran out, a light would come on, and it would take around forty-five seconds for the next litre to be ready. The downside was that it was a bit of a handful, the upside was clean, hot water. It was amazing what a difference a wash can make after days without one. Gus, who had been scooting for hours, looked black from the dust, and his hair was starting to resemble dreadlocks. We sat him in the bucket and gave him a good scrub.

All washed up, we took the long stroll through the RUHSA grounds and out the front to the K Paul Hotel for dinner. Of course Gus brought his scooter, and again the kids ran up and down with him as he scooted between two speed humps around forty metres apart. The rest of us had an evening coffee before we sat for dinner. The hotel, with its small and assorted wooden tables and benches, was an experience just to sit in. Paul, as always, stood at his bench waiting for his clientele to arrive, and shooed the street dogs out as we walked in. The menu was chapatti and potato curry with a tomato chutney – a specialty and one of our favourites. Subashini told us that her parents would often work 4 am to 8 pm seven days a week. After dinner, we arranged for Christopher to take the kids for a night ride on his motorbike. Even Bec and Kate had a ride, and Gus and Max said it was the highlight of their trip. I knew how they felt. I had enjoyed my trips out with Christopher when I visited in 2005. He would take me to the markets, the tailors, and wherever else I needed to go.

Afterwards we came together for the family photos. I was especially happy to get a photo with Paul. I felt humbled by this proud man who worked so hard for his family. Paul's brother joined us just in time for goodbyes. He hugged everyone, smiling from ear to ear, so happy to see us. He brought joy with him everywhere he went. We managed to slip Paul some money for dinner, which of course he initially refused. They had been so generous to us for the past few days, and we were all very grateful to have been together as two complete families for the first time. As we strolled back to our rooms, Bec and I shared our gratitude of being in the presence of such a wonderful family, who provided us with an experience that we would never forget.

Day 29 RUHSA to Vellore

The plan for day twenty-nine was for the walk team to start walking from RUHSA to Vellore, and for the support team to drive ahead and find accommodation. This was the first day we set off without our accommodation organised, so we were a little anxious about what would be waiting at the other end. We had to be packed and ready to leave by 7.30 am in an attempt to beat the heat of the Indian day, which was a big effort. To put this in perspective, as Indy and I were getting dressed, Gus was rolling around in our bed and drinking his tea, not too keen to go anywhere, and Maggie was dead to the world. I think she could sleep through just about anything. Bec had done a great job packing the day before, but there were always so many little things still to organise when you travel with a family, and it is fair to say the pressure was on. Kate, the kids and Nanna and Poppa were ready and knocking on our door set to go – a great effort considering the state of their room the night before.

The walk team consisted of Kate, Ally and Maxy, Nick, Indy, Maggie and myself. It was a big team, and despite the early start, the temperature was already starting to rise. Apart from that, the walk conditions were very good, given we had some cloud cover and tree shade along the route. The kids found it hard going, however, with a couple of mini meltdowns early on in the piece from Ally and Maxy, while Maggie was requiring pretty constant attention to keep her focused and moving forward. For an adult on the walk team, it was pretty much one hundred per cent kid focused – as Kate attested to after her first few days. As often happened on our walks, the team broke into smaller groups just to rotate the energy and attention for the kids, but for Kate, Poppa and me there was little rest.

I'm sure most of you can imagine what it would be like to set off on a twenty-five-kilometre walk with kids, but if you can't, by all means pack up tomorrow and set off. You would probably find your kids – like ours – complaining of hunger and injury, and asking how much longer it will take in the first ten minutes of the journey. Walks often take longer, as you are walking at a slower pace, and in conditions over thirty degrees it is even harder. If you are really keen, then you can get up and do it all over again the next day, and the day after that. Our experience was that it was much more of a mental game than a physical one, and our kids were quite capable of walking the distance.

When we stopped for a rest I gave the kids a hydrolyte drink to avoid dehydration. They enjoyed these stops, and it gave them more energy to keep going. We walked around fifteen kilometres to a town called Katpadi and found Raju waiting. Ally, Max and Maggie were in the van before I had the chance to say, 'Have you guys had enough?' Indy, Poppa, Kate and I continued the final seven kilometres to Vellore – a large town, well known for the Christian Medical College and Hospital that had strong ties with Australia.

It had been a long, hot walk – as I suspected all would be from here on in. Raju drove us back to our hotel – only a few hundred metres from where we stopped. Seemed a bit silly when it was so close, but Raju was not to be deterred from fulfilling his daily duties. Unfortunately we could only find somewhere to accommodate us for one evening, and it was likely that we would need to stay in town for three nights – accommodation being very difficult to come by and organise in advance. Mum and Bec did a great job finding our lodgings, and we arrived to see Gus riding his scooter around the marble hallways on the third floor. There was a great drop to the ground floor. The rooms were built on each of four sides of the hotel with a large open courtyard in the middle. On the corner of each floor there were steps built into the wall – perfect for Gus to climb and look down on the fishpond below. It looked like we were going to have to keep a very close eye on the little man. Bec managed to organise a family room, so we all had a bed – a nice change from recent days. I settled Gus down for an afternoon sleep; something we were fast learning was an essential element to a successful day. The rest of the kids ordered up some room service – chicken tikka and naan seemed to be the highlight. I ordered some vegetarian noodles, which were a nice change from the curries. We headed out for a short walk when Gus woke up, gave the kids a massage to iron out any sore spots, did a spot of reading, and called it a night. Bec and I decided on coffee and biscuits instead of dinner; a mistake we wouldn't make again as we were up until 3 am before we could get to sleep.

Day 30 Vellore to Ranipet

Mum and Kate kindly offered to look after Gus to enable Bec to join in for part of the walk. Maggie, Ally and Maxy decided on a rest day after a big effort the day before, so Indy, Kate, Poppa and I started the day. The walk out of Vellore was mostly along a highway, so there wasn't a lot to report. We walked for a couple of hours without a break, and were looking for a spot to stop for a drink when Raju pulled up with Bec who swapped with Kate. We were excited to see that Ally and Maggie decided to walk the last ten kilometres of their own volition.

It was the first day where we struggled to find a rest stop. We walked along for an additional two hours on a hot and dusty major highway. Not a lot of fun. The kids were pretty good, and kept themselves distracted by talking about things they were looking forward to when they got home – including rearranging their rooms. We had been walking for four hours without a stop, and were feeling fatigued. Fortunately, Nick and I found a couple of small shops down a side lane, and stocked up on cold water and a packet of chips. We swore to be better prepared for the next day. The next half an hour wasn't too bad, although for the first time my feet were starting to feel sore, and Indy had a few leg pains. We pushed on regardless, and found Raju waiting for us at the edge of Ranipet. Poppa grilled Raju about where the town actually was, to which he replied, 'It is here.' Poppa continued to push, and Raju gestured over the bridge that stood in front of us. Indy was keen to get in the van, but wouldn't let Poppa and

I finish the walk without her. With obvious frustration, she stepped out and huffed and puffed up the road. Happy with their efforts, Maggie and Ally jumped in the van, deciding near enough was good enough. It turned out that we only had another 500 metres to walk across the bridge, and found Raju waiting for us. Poppa was very satisfied to finish the walk. Indy wasn't quite as happy.

We headed back to the hotel to hear that Kate, Mum, Gus and Maxy had enjoyed a restful day. Mum was sitting typing her blog, and Gussy was asleep – a little earlier than usual. We ordered lunch and Gus woke up just in time for his French fries and fruit salad. The girls had their usual. I headed down to the lobby to quickly check a few emails, and on the way back saw Kate heading out with the big kids. I could hear Gus screaming from the lobby as Kate looked at me and suggested Bec might need a hand. Sure enough, the little man was in the middle of a major meltdown. Thirty days on the road was taking its toll. It took a good few minutes, a cup of tea, and a book to settle him down. Nanna and Poppa came over soon after, and Gus took a great deal of enjoyment in shaving Poppa's head with the electric razor. Bec and I then took him for a quick walk to buy some supplies. He had decided that chewing gum was really cool – something I'm sure he got off Maxy – so he was on a mission, and took great delight in finding some.

When we arrived back at the hotel we had a quick meeting with the whole team, as we had heard that a film crew would be joining us for the next walk leg. .As always, we encouraged the kids to be natural and honest, and asked them a few questions to help them think about how they might respond to the media. They were whipped into a frenzy, each in good spirits as they tried to out do the other with their answers. So much so that Maggie ended up on her feet, incorporating a bit of song and dance.

The kids ordered up their chicken tikka, fries, and naan bread while Bec and I decided on a cup of tea for dinner. We were in bed early as usual. The days were long, and a good night's sleep was important – especially after the lack of sleep the night before. We soon had a knock on the door from Kate, who had been checking Facebook in the lobby. She had heard an alarm sound, and looked up to see the glass elevator stuck between floors. Sure enough, there was Max in the elevator – looking very sheepish – having pressed the STOP button. The temptation to experiment was too strong, and he had succumbed – only to find out that the stopping was permanent. As staff came running to get him out of the lift, Kate just lowered her gaze and typed a little note about the incident on Facebook. Max was at last released and he put his head down, avoided Kate's eyes, and ran upstairs to bed.

Day 31 Ranipet to Kaveripakkam

The good night's sleep we had hoped for was not to be. It sounded like construction works were going on next door, but later investigation revealed we were directly under a bar. India woke up a little cranky (a lot cranky), and was rabbiting on about lodging a formal complaint with management. She was quickly becoming accustomed to the Indian way. The biggest shock was that Bec, aka Nurse Ratchet, aka the soul and rock of the family, was sick. As the night went on, her cold further developed, and she awoke with what felt like a full-blown flu. Having taken the time to look after everyone else, she had forgotten about herself. As many of you would understand, nurses are not particularly good patients, and she was taking direction somewhat reluctantly. We were all a little slow as we headed down for an early breakfast of omelettes and toast. Gus had some pineapple juice, and then decided he was sick of this sitting thing. I decided to take him back to the room to spare the others, and we shared a bowl of honey loops back in our room – the breakfast of champions!

There was an anxious feeling in the bus as all ten of us left the hotel, as we weren't sure what the day would involve. We had been given a brief of the types of questions we were likely to be asked, but none of us had worked with a film crew before. We arrived at the agreed meeting point I had found on Google Maps – or so I thought. We all got out of the car as it was getting increasingly stuffy, and at only 9 am there was a sting in the sun; we could tell it was going to be a hot one. We sat and waited by the car on a busy corner, traffic cruising by, again looking somewhat out of place. The sun was so hot that we were sweating just standing still. Flies covered us head to toe. The bus was no relief, as they had found their way in there as well. Mum decided to use the toilet at a nearby hotel, and immediately regretted her decision, as she later described it as the worst toilet she had ever seen or smelt. Gus was running around like a madman; his shorts and shirt soon drenched with sweat. The big kids were suffering in not so much silence, and shared every detail of their discomfort. We couldn't start walking, as we were unsure what route the crew would want to take, so we were stuck with the heat and the flies. Not such a great start to the day, but another chance to practice our patience and tolerance.

After several animated telephone calls with Raju, and what seemed like an eternity, the crew finally arrived. We were keen to get moving, so after some quick introductions, we clarified directions and set off. After a walk along the highway the day before, we were pleased to see this route took us on a road that ran parallel to the highway and through the shopping district. It was as if the day was scripted; young kids came up to us and said hello, a man on a motorbike with his very young son stopped for a chat, and then returned minutes later with a handful of chocolate bars for Gus. I wasn't sure if it was the camera, but we seemed to be attracting even more attention than usual. Now that I think about it, it was definitely the camera.

Gus started off in the stroller, then moved to my shoulders, was carried, ran along the side of the road, and became a plane. He was very busy. We stopped by a temple for some shade and a drink. The kids were sitting on a concrete table, which we were told was okay, but that they needed to keep their feet off. As you can imagine, as soon as I told Gus, all he wanted to do was put his shoes on the bench. I distracted him with the option to make a donation to the temple, which he was happy to do. We walked along for another hour or so before we decided that the heat was too much for the larger team, and everyone jumped into the bus, except Kate, Poppa and me. Indy was having an enforced rest day after the long and very hot walk the day before. We wanted to ensure that she finished the walk in the same state that she started it. If we didn't force her to rest, her stubbornness would see her walk herself into injury. I wonder where she got that trait?

The bus stayed close by as the crew wanted to do a couple of interviews with the kids. The three walkers continued on, stopped for a morning coffee despite the heat, and enjoyed the scenery. The coffee stop was in the usual galvanized leaning roof, with an old bench and boiling milk on the go. There was a large crowd gathered at the bench, something we assumed was a good sign, and we all stood around enjoying our coffee. Nick was soon finished with his plastic cup, and asked one of the men what he should do with it – thinking there would be a bin nearby. The other man grabbed it and dropped it on the ground. It reminded us of the time we were travelling by train on another trip to India, and Mum very conscientiously collected all of our rubbish, put it in a bag, and tied it up. She approached one of the train staff and handed it to him, and to her surprise, he threw it out of the train.

I shared a few more words with some of the people standing around, although they looked a little disinterested when I started to talk about the cricket scores. Michael Clarke's 250 not out in the recent test meant Australia was on top once again, much to the disappointment of the fanatical Indian fans. We continued on through a town called Walajapet – clearly a cane paradise – and Kate was drooling at all of the beautiful cane pieces displayed in nearby windows. She was very keen to take them home to her own shop. From there on the day was a solid walk for the three of us, while the kids had some time with the film crew. They found a small school and enjoyed playtime with the students before being interviewed. A couple of them got stuck when asked, 'Do you think you will do something like this again?' Indy was ready though, and had plans for our next adventure. Apparently Gus was a little shy when it came to his turn; very un-Gus like.

We completed another solid twenty-four kilometres in hot conditions – a good effort particularly considering the morning was slow. In the end we made it past our final destination, and pushed out a few extra kilometres. The mood in the car on the way back to the hotel, and our final night in Vellore, was surprisingly good considering Bec, Mum and the kids had been in the car for over three hours. Bec was looking tired, and enjoyed a quiet moment at the back of the bus after another long day.

We had a quiet lunch back at the room, a few games with the kids, and an early night.

Day 32
Kaveripakkam toward Chennai

Day thirty-two marked another pack-up and rest day for the kids. Bec was back to her usual self; nothing could keep Big Mama down for long. She had packed all the bags, and as always, did an amazing job at getting us ready. Learning from the day before, I stayed with Gus in our room until Bec finished breakfast and took over babysitting duties. I enjoyed another plain breakfast of an omelette and banana, and looked across to Indy's plate to see it filled with potato curry, a vada, a poori, and coconut chutney. This was the girl who didn't like spice when we left for India.

Over breakfast the great man Sachin Tendulkar was dismissed, resulting in many groans from the mainly Indian contingent in the restaurant. After a quick breakfast, we grabbed our bags and got into the van. Raju dropped Poppa and me at the spot we finished the day before, and we noted that we were less than a hundred kilometres away from our final destination of Chennai. We bid farewell to the rest of the crew as they headed off to find our next accommodation spot around fifty kilometres up the road.

After a short while I turned to Nick and said, 'Well we have broken the back of it now, Nick. Short of an unforeseen event we are there.' Not fifteen metres up the road we heard the sound of screeching brakes, and turned to see a car with locked brakes skidding to narrowly avoid a motorbike that had cut in front of it. The car, with little control, smashed into the median strip –which in India was a concrete barrier nearly a foot high. As it smashed, its wheel guard broke off and flew across the road, hitting the car coming in the opposite direction. The motorcyclist, clearly the cause of the accident, wasted no time in taking off across the highway and down a side road. The passengers stepped out, somewhat dazed but not hurt, and inspected the extensive damage to their car. We waited long enough to make sure everyone was okay, and then continued on with our walk and conversation.

'Now as I was saying, Poppa,' I continued, 'We are nearly there!'

It was a timely reminder to stay focused until the very end.

Poppa and I made good time and pushed out nearly six kilometres each hour. We decided to walk against the traffic, as there was a little bit of shade every now and then. Gestures from a few drivers suggested that we should be walking on the other side of the road. It appeared to be fine for any type of vehicle to drive down the wrong side of the road, but not two pedestrians. Unperturbed, we pressed on and enjoyed the shade. Nick and I shared a few words, but were happy to appreciate the quietness of the day without a larger team. We had a few quick stops for water, and then a final one for a cold Fanta by the side of the road. We soon came across a small crowd gathering. Nick wondered aloud if it was a favourite 'Pee Stop', but as we drew closer we noticed a large truck, laden with bricks, upside-down off the side of the road. The accident must have happened last night, and it appeared as though the driver had fallen asleep and driven down the embankment – although this was just a guess.

We were back in the car with Raju when we witnessed something to mark the end of a day of near misses. Two men decided to walk their motorcycle in front of the fast oncoming traffic on the highway. They were in the middle of the right hand lane when they seemed to stall their bike. The truck in front of us veered left, and stopped in the middle of the road. We were travelling much faster than it, and so didn't have time to slow down. I saw Raju glance in his mirrors to see what was coming from behind as we swerved – narrowly avoiding the truck. All we could hear was the sound of brakes screeching behind us, and we hoped that all made it through in one piece. I asked Raju if everyone was okay, and he gestured 'Yes' with a head wobble; clearly a little shaken after the ordeal.

We returned to the hotel, and were pleasantly surprised by the quality of our new accommodation. The rooms were spacious, with extra beds available, and there was a large pool for the kids complete with blue water. Everyone had a swim and a cool down after another extremely hot day. Gus and I had an early meal, and headed to bed at around 5.30 pm – both exhausted after our day. The girls enjoyed dinner with Kate and the kids, and then finally hit the hay around 8.30 pm. Indy started to complain about her hard mattress and the fact that she couldn't get her hips straight. This woke up Gus who was in the bed with us, and as I was settling him back to sleep I felt a wet patch. Maybe a puddle is more accurate. Gus, who was wearing an Indian nappy, had somehow managed to miss it completely, and find the bed. Bec grabbed a couple of towels, we covered up the wet patch, and back to sleep we went.

Day 33 Fifty-five kilometres to Chennai

The big kids were all back on board, and Mum happily accepted another opportunity to have Gus to herself, which meant Bec could join the walk team. The accommodation we had was much more conducive to Gus, with plenty of room to scooter, a park and an empty pond. The pond was like a toddler's skate park, and Gus had a great time pulling all sorts of manoeuvres as he scooted around. It kept him busy for hours. The plan was for the kids and Bec to walk ten kilometres and call it a day. I had a quick look at the walk plan, and noted that Maggie had already completed over 160 kilometres, with two walks over twenty-five kilometres. It was a great effort for a nine-year-old. She would complete over 200 kilometres before we finished. She had definitely been our 'surprise packet' on the walk, given we weren't sure how much walking she would do, and we were very proud of her.

The walk into Chennai was a little uninspiring, as we were walking along a boring main highway, and only interacting with the occasional waving motorist. One of the things we miss least about India is the sound of blowing horns, which were often used as a status symbol, and the louder the horn the better. Every vehicle made a point of tooting as they drove past – regardless of the traffic, or how close to the road we were. The drivers – so many of whom were driving the same brand that it seemed to be the year of the Hyundai – noted our uniqueness and made a special effort to ensure we noticed them. How could we not?

The kids found the ten-kilometre, two-hour walk very manageable, and there were limited complaints. Maxy was the first member of our walk team to christen the Indian-style squat. Kate commented that it was the same colour as the multiple others she had seen, so he must have been eating the right food. It was only right that he should squat on this leg of the walk, as moments before Bec had named the road the Faeces Stretch, as it seemed to be well adorned with all manner of landmines from all sorts of creatures.

As per usual, Ally nearly knocked down a few of us on her way to the van once Raju arrived, although I must say she did a great job on the walk. The lure of her cousins was too great for Maggie, and she and Bec also retired for the day. The hotel was only five to six kilometres away, so Indy decided to push through and complete the walk with Kate, Poppa and me. We made it back quite early, and decided to set up for a nice lunch of butter chicken and vegetable curry with naan and take advantage of the extra time we had together to relax. The food on the trip had been spectacular from the dodgiest looking place to the finer restaurants. At one stage we were worried that we would return home ten kilograms heavier, but fortunately, a little illness went a long way, and as we picked up the walking the weight steadily dropped off. Phew!

To finish our day today I thought I would share a section from Indy's journal (with her blessing of course). She is a very inspiring young woman, my daughter.

Indy's Journal
My Big Hairy Audacious Goal for 2011

So I'm sitting in the Singapore airport with my family waiting for my connecting flight to Kochi, India, and I am thinking, how the hell did I get here? How did I go from feeling sorry for the people living in poverty, to walking 800 kilometres in six weeks across India? What brought me here? The simple answer is Dad. He came up with the idea to raise money for disadvantaged children and families. He was the all-inspiring reason I was the first to sign up to be a part of the full-time walk team, the reason I chose to give to others as I am given to myself. Another reason is that I am simply trying to make myself deserving of the wonderful and leisurely life I have been so kindly given. Another key piece of the puzzle is my amazing mutti (Mum) who gets me back on track when it all becomes too much and I have a mental breakdown. She reminds me why I do what I do, and helps me when I am broken and need fixing. She's my rock, and Dad's my inspiration. I need one just as much as I need the other. So back to how I'm sitting in the Singapore airport with my family, as much as this is just a pointless moment out of infinity in time, it is the moment I set off for one of the biggest journeys of my life. I say 'one of' because judging by the conversations on our training walk, this won't be the last (huge) adventure. This is the 'Mooch' signing off for now but not for long. I have fifty days of journal writing ahead of me! Gotta go catch a plane to India!

Indy's Journal
Day 8
Mysore Village – Top of the 'Best Experiences' List

Today we went to a welcome in a small community in Mysore, and visited a village where some of the funds we raised are going. I raised money for twenty-eight (and still counting) bicycles for young girls, to help them get to different places safely (like school). After the welcome around a hundred kids walked eight kilometres with us. It was amazing holding hands and talking with all of them. They only knew how to say, 'How are you?' and, 'I am fine,' and, 'My name is …' and, 'What is your name?' but just having photos with them, and looking into their beautiful faces was enough for me to be able to understand the double meaning and true thanks of their words. All the children kept telling me how beautiful I was yet I was almost jealous of their extraordinary faces and big eyes. I feel so lucky to have an experience like that, it was one of the best days of my life.

Indy's Journal
Day 10
Blessing Ceremony

I felt like a celebrity walking down the red carpet. ChildFund India had set up a huge hall filled with 500 people and flowers and candles everywhere. It was beautiful. We walked to the stage as a family. The room was filled and the ceremony started. There was a prayer dance and four girls danced in reddish, pink and orange dresses, with loads of jewels and make up. They looked extraordinary. There was a handing out of flowers and a few plays from other kids. Different people talked including the Bishop of Mysore. The best part was at the end when I got to do an impromptu speech and give out the bicycles I had raised money for. It was excellent seeing the extremely grateful look on the girls' faces as I presented them with their bicycles. The press took photos of every single one and I cried because I was so happy and proud of it all.

Indy's Journal
Day 13
Snake Valley

The walk today was probably the most fun and eventful of them all. About a kilometre into the walk and we met a boy with his fly zipper on his pants undone. Three kilometres in and Dad and Poppa had their heads shaved! I was going, 'No, no!' the whole time, but I am slowly getting used to it after thirteen years of my dad having the same haircut. Anyway, about nine kilometres into the walk, Dad was looking for a big stick to walk with, saw a long blackish, brown one, bent down to pick it up and then, only when it scampered at the speed of light into the bushes, did he realise it was a snake! He yelled, 'Uh, snake!' and we all just about had a heart attack. Eibhlin yelled, 'F*&$', Mum jumped so high I thought she was levitating, and Poppa yelled in a very high-pitched, girlish voice, 'What is it? What is it? What is it?' It was hilarious once we knew it was gone, and it hadn't bitten anyone. Had my first chocolate (Cadbury) in ages with a pineapple juice. Eibhlin gave me a leg and a foot rub and I was 'yelling' so much that I sounded like a yapping dog.

Day 34
Thirty kilometres to Chennai

As I awoke at around 6 am I could hear quiet sniffles and groans coming from Bec in the bed below. Having had a swim the day before, her body had succumbed again to the lurgy she was so desperately trying to avoid. She had a fairly sleepless night with a throbbing head and blocked sinuses – no fun for Nurse Ratchet. Master Gus had awoken and was already ordering his cup tea from Dadda, sensing that Mum was not a good candidate. We didn't have milk, so I used the creamer and made it too hot – not a good start for the little man. We planned to leave early as we could start our walk straight from the hotel. Early mornings were never good for Miss Maggie, who was difficult to rouse at 10 am, so the 6.30 am wake-up call was fraught with danger. Indy had a few gurgles in her stomach the night before so was also a little sluggish, but very determined to walk.

As always, Kate and her kids were up, dressed, and ready for breakfast well before us. Kate had been doing an awesome job as a single mum with two kids on their first trip to India. Ally and Maxy approached their trip in very different ways. Maxy dived in headfirst, eating everything, keen to walk and open to all that he could experience. Ally was a little older and therefore a little more cautious. Having a spice phobia also changed her experience. Kate had been patient, tolerant, and supportive of not only her kids, but also the rest of the team, while trying to have an experience of her own. Nice job, little sis!

Gus was up and headed out to the pool with nothing but his nappy on. This was a concern given that he had decided to jump in fully clothed without floaties only the day before. We were now on round-the-clock surveillance of the little man. We slowly got dressed. Maggie needed some extra encouragement to firstly open her eyes, then get dressed, and then get to breakfast. We had accepted that she just was not a morning person. Mags had also secured a new nickname. In recent trips to India she had become known as Maggie Noodles – after Maggi Noodles. That week, one of the camera crew named Maggie 'Two Minutes', which we thought was a crack-up.

We had a plain but enriching breakfast of a couple of fried eggs on toast and cornflakes. The plan was for the kids to walk for around two hours, while Kate, Poppa and I would walk an extra three to push out twenty-five kilometres. Mum had once again offered to have Gus, which made Bec even more upset as she was missing out on a potential walk day. We made good time, and the kids were pushing out around five kilometres an hour. Ally and Maxy had settled into their walk routine well, but Maxy seemed to have his body clock a little out of whack, and had to stop again for a squat. We found a fence for him to go behind, but there was a gap between the two sheets of galvanised iron. Given it was at waist height, young Maxy put on quite a show for the walk team. I suggested he needed to get some sun on his butt cheeks! I had recently shared that I was thankful that the 'poo shovel' we had packed for emergencies had not been out of the bag yet. Maybe I spoke too soon.

The walk continued with the kids benefiting from constant stories, discussion about home, and the old faithful twenty questions, which involved questions about life such as, 'What is your favourite food?', 'What will you do when you grow up?', and, 'What is your favourite holiday?' Indy, who we decided would only walk the two hours, was having an internal debate about whether or not to continue. She had been having a small problem with her leg, and I knew she would struggle with the last five to ten kilometres. Being such a stubborn little lady, she would die trying to make the finish line. I made the decision for her to finish early with the other kids, and it took a few kilometres for the Mooch to stop mooching and understand it was in her best interest. Fortunately she came around, and we had a nice chat before the end of her walk.

The kids rotated well between Kate, Nick and me, so we managed to get them to the 10 am pick up time. For the first time on the walk, however, there was no Raju, and no car waiting for us. This sent Ally into a bit of a meltdown, as I think she had her mind, heart and soul set on the fact that she would be picked up at precisely the right time – which to be fair is what happened on previous days. She did not deal with the fact that we had to keep walking all that well, but we managed to push on for an additional twenty minutes and clear another couple of kilometres. Once Raju arrived, Ally didn't spot him right away, and continued to drag her heels – looking half dead on her feet. When she heard the word she has been dreaming about – 'Raju' – she ran like a gazelle to the van, almost knocking Kate down in the process. Ally and Maxy did a great job and, aside from the little meltdown at the end, walked with good energy and spirit. Mags the Trooper could have walked all day as long as she had someone to talk to, and again proved herself to be a champion contributor to the walk team.

Meanwhile, back at the hotel, Bec and Nanna were enjoying breakfast while Gus was in capable hands elsewhere. Apparently one of the wonderful ladies at the hotel offered to look after our little man while Bec finished breakfast. She looked out at one stage and Gus had six of the hotel staff waiting on his every need. He had a milkshake, juice, pancakes and anything else a three-year-old superstar might desire. He then took great enjoyment in helping the ladies arrange flowers in the water display, and placed every flower in the water – getting all the colours in order. The ladies were lovely and patient, and kept him in peaceful play for a long time. Bec regarded it as a very special memory, and thinks of it fondly to this day.

Meanwhile, Kate, Nick and I were charging on, and after five hours pushed out twenty-five kilometres. We only had a couple of quick stops for 7 Up and roadside coffee. Other than that it was a straightforward, highway walk. The similarities to Tailem Bend and Port Wakefield – both popular trucking towns in South Australia with dry, dusty highways – were remarkable.

I (the classic introverted feeler) had disappeared into my 'man cave' in the previous couple of days. For a variety of small reasons I had lost a little of the glow I had earlier in the walk, which wouldn't have been good at the best of times, and especially not then given I was leading the team. I used to disappear into myself for days at a time; not always knowing how to work my way through the various feelings I was processing. It was thanks to discussions with Bec that I started being able to snap out of them quite quickly. Fortunately for everyone, this time was no different, and she told it to me straight – suggesting I pull my head in. Bec, who was reading this as I typed, suggested she had been a little more subtle – although that is up for debate. Regardless, I was happy for the help and direction provided by the true leader of our team.

We were only days away from the end of our incredible adventure, and wanted to take every opportunity to have more of the experiences that typified our coast-to-coast walk.

Day 35 Walk to Ambattur

We had another early start given the film crew would be arriving at the hotel at 7.30 am. As I awoke I checked for signs of life. Indy recovered well after complaining of stomach cramps before bed, Bec had a good night's sleep but was still feeling unwell, Gus was happy and ordering up his cup tea, and Maggie slept in with her cousins last night so there was no need to go through the waking routine with her. The film crew arrived exactly at 7.30 am, which was very unusual for India, but a welcome change. Nanna and Poppa were interviewed first in the gardens, while Gus sat outside on the swing with pancakes and maple syrup. It seemed to be the best way to get him to sit still long enough to eat something.

Bec was next. As Kate and I watched from a distance, we noticed that she and Gus had the same hand actions in front of the camera. We weren't quite sure who learnt it from whom. Bec was determined to show up and speak from the heart, rather than try and script anything, in order to tell her story with the highest integrity. After Bec it was Indy's turn, and she was such a cool cucumber. At only thirteen years of age, she was an incredible role model for other young girls. I went next, and like Bec, I wanted to convey the essence of what the adventure had been about. My issue was that whenever I spoke about my family, I always got very emotional, and that day was no different. Kate followed me, and then Poppa had a second go on his own. Meanwhile the day was steadily getting hotter, and the hours were flying by. Of course the kids were getting hungry. We ordered up some fries as an early lunch, and it was 11.30 am before we finally got on the road.

We walked from our finish spot the day before – thirty kilometres out of Chennai. We planned to walk within fifteen kilometres of Chennai, near to Ambattur, a small, urban town. The plan from there was to have a symbolic finish with ChildFund the next day, and then come back and finish the last twenty kilometres of our walk to the Chennai coastline at Marina Beach after that. The walk team included everybody but Bec, Mum and Gus. We toyed with the idea of Bec and Gus doing a short walk, but the route was along a busy, hot and dusty highway that could be quite dangerous. The verge was quite narrow in places, and large trucks and buses drove along at great speed. It was not a good combination with Gus. Instead, they went ahead to secure the accommodation. We gave ourselves three hours to complete the fifteen kilometres, which would be fine – albeit a solid walk with four kids.

Luckily, they were in the zone. They took it upon themselves to chat together, and had plenty to talk about to pass the time. The camera crew followed us on our way, and found it to be quite a challenge to keep up. They were lovely men, and told us that it was an unusual assignment for them given they were used to still shots and interviews at one location, rather than following their target fifteen kilometres down a highway.

We stopped for soft drinks and chips to recharge the kids, who didn't complain once the whole day. This was especially impressive given our walk was anything but picturesque. We either had to walk on the bitumen verge closer to the highway, or on a dirt track near the verge, which was heavily undulated and gave our calves a good workout. As always, there were all manner of sights to see. Cows were sitting in the middle of the highway, vehicles were driving on the wrong side of the road, and oxen were pulling carts. Then a BMW X5 cruised by – we never knew what we would be seeing next. It was easy after all that time to be complacent about the wondrous views that surrounded us, so every now and again we stopped to soak it all in. We eventually made our way to a service road next to the highway. It was only two lanes wide. One lane was taken up completely by parked trucks, while the other was covered with ankle-deep sand and dirt, with large trucks driving up from behind us and whirling the dust into our faces.

At one point the journalist suggested we sing a song to celebrate our arrival into a town called Poonamallee.

The adults suggested 'Advance Australia Fair' or 'Waltzing Matilda', but the kids weren't very keen on that idea. We ended up with an impromptu, 'Give me a P, P. Give me an O, O'. I think you get the drift. To finish off, I sang, 'Where are we?' to which the group repeated in unison, 'I don't know.' Not bad for something we made up on the spot. The song fired up the kids, and for the next forty-five minutes they loudly sang a complete rendition of all our family songs, smiles beaming on their faces. Kate and I suggested that it would be good if Nick could compose some more culturally and venue appropriate tunes for the kids on the next trip, given one of the favourites was 'Grubby Little Wombat'. He made up a 'Walking to Chennai' song on the spot, that they quickly learnt and continued to sing in full voice.

We comfortably made it through the three hours, and the kids were still going strong at the finish line. Once again when Ally spotted Raju, she leapt to a sprint – almost topping the land speed record for a twelve-year-old. In the van she commented that it was the first day she felt she could have kept walking. The best walker award was definitely shared by all four kids that day. We had very hot and difficult conditions, but there was not one complaint. Wonderful job, kids.

We jumped into the van and finally made it from the highway to the city sprawl, heading into Chennai peak hour as we went. We soon realised it would have been quicker to walk. It took an hour to drive the ten kilometres to our hotel on the road we had been walking along the whole time. It was in the heart of Chennai, and I had the immediate feeling it was not going to be a good stay. We were back into a normal hotel room, with no space for Gus to run or play. It was going to be a long three days. Fortunately we had a very busy time ahead, as we would be finishing our time with ChildFund and our walk.

Gus had his third little meltdown in forty-five minutes as he coped with the walls being a little closer than he was used to. Bec shared with me that Gus and Raju had a new game, where they would pull funny faces at each other when Gus got into the bus. Gus wouldn't let anyone but Raju put his seatbelt on, and I was unsure how Gus would cope with saying goodbye to his new, special friend.

The kids ordered up their dinner – Maggie excitedly choosing the pizza. Unfortunately it resembled an explosion of grilled cheese on a flat bit of bread more than anything else, and the taste was difficult to describe. It would have been best to stick to the naan I think! Bec and I shared a lovely chicken dish and some aloo jeera. Bec was still far from a hundred per cent, and we hoped that she would have a good night's sleep. We had two double beds here so Gus, Bec and I slept in one, and the girls in the other. Indy was very happy to be off the floor at last.

Day 36
Community Walk and Symbolic ChildFund Finish

The day started as usual. Indy was up and getting herself ready, Gus was on his scooter with just a nappy on looking for trouble, and Maggie groaned from her bed, waiting until the last minute to get up. Bec was upright but still showing the effects of her cold. She was determined to make it through the day, and wouldn't even think of staying home to rest. After breakfast, we saw the friendly and smiling faces of our friends Naomi, Sachal, Dola and of course Antony. The team was going to walk the final three kilometres of our journey with us to the office of a ChildFund partner called Kalaiselvi Karunalaya Social Welfare Society (KKSS), an NGO based in Ambattur. We drove a short distance from the hotel and saw a crowd of around thirty people holding green signs. In the crowd were ten police officers to act as our escorts through the busy Indian streets.

We wasted no time getting into formation, and got ready to begin our final steps with ChildFund. The kids were brought to full volume by Antony, who was chanting, 'ChildFund India. We are for children.' As we walked, the meaning of each step was not lost on the team, despite the hot conditions. Our journey started thirty-five days before in the same way; walking with ChildFund people on the west coast of India. And there we were again with the

ChildFund team, and many other wonderful ChildFund supporters, getting closer and closer to the finish line.

The walk was a short one, and before we knew it we were turning into the ChildFund office, to once again be greeted by a sea of smiling children's faces that were awaiting our arrival. We could not have asked for a better welcome, or finish to our walk. We enjoyed some tea and biscuits, and then Antony and the staff introduced us to the ChildFund sponsorship process. It was very interesting for the kids to learn how ChildFund identified the most deprived, vulnerable, and excluded children, and enrolled one child per family – although the sponsorship benefited the whole family, and in many cases the broader community in which the child lived. This talk was also preparing us for a visit to a local community the next day, where we intended to start sponsoring a child.

We headed to a short presentation to mark the end of our walk, and provide further items to local children and families. By this time, Gus had found a very small playground outside the office with two swings – one partially broken – and a slide. Trying to encourage him to stay away from the playground was a big ask, and eventually I had to carry him up the stairs to the presentation. He was very unhappy with this decision and made sure I knew it. As I sat in the presentation room trying to take in the moment and say hello to some of the kids, Gus unloaded a barrage of free hits on any part of my face or body that he could find. It wasn't a great way to start the event, but the show had to go on. We were invited to light the five wicks on the commemorative candle. This at last caught Gus' attention and he started to calm down. Each of the kids took it in turns lighting one of the wicks, and we all tried to stop Gus from blowing them out as we had in Mysore several weeks before.

There were a couple of short speeches introducing our team, and what we had been doing in India. Dola from ChildFund spoke generously about our efforts, and I was then asked to say a few words. As is usually the case, Gus had been asking when was it his turn, and decided to go first. Unfortunately he was too short to see over the top of the podium, so we tried standing him on the podium but that didn't work either. He was eventually handed a roaming microphone and he was away. He introduced everyone in the team, including noting that his Poppa was a 'swing maniac' – a name Gus had come up with after a recent trip to the park. He talked about money for goats, our driver Raju, and his home in Mount Martha. He of course had everyone in the room hanging off his every word, and was quite the entertainer. I am sure there were groans of disappointment when I had to intervene and suggested it was my turn.

I spoke quickly about our journey, and the wonderfully warm and friendly hospitality we encountered every step of the way. I talked about why we were doing the walk, and what we hoped to achieve, and then decided to do something impromptu – which is usually never a good idea. I asked for five kids from the audience to come up and stand with our five kids, and spoke about the fact that we believed every child was special, and that they deserved to be safe, healthy and going to school, no matter where they were from. I wasn't sure if the point was made well or not, but it was at the heart of our drive to support kids all around the world. I always wondered what it must be like for families to lose their children, given approximately 24,000 children under the age of five die a day. I thought about how much we loved Gus, how he was such an important part of our family, and what impact it would have if we were to lose him. This would be no different for other families. Many mothers carried their babies for nine months, struggled to nourish and care for them, and then watched them die from something preventable, such as diarrhoea or a chest infection. Just because these families were in another country didn't mean it should carry any less meaning or importance. Yet this was happening every day, and it was happening on our watch. It was something we wanted to put right.

After the speeches, we started giving out gifts to the children – the thing we had most been looking forward to. The girls were each presented with a key to their bikes, and our kids lined up to distribute them. In total we distributed twenty bikes, ten water filters, eighty mosquito nets, and a hundred school kits. Only a few of the school kits were distributed; the rest of the children received a token, and would receive their kits at the end of the presentation. I asked if it would be okay for our kids to distribute them. Indy, Ally, Maggie and Max were lost in the crowd as kids lined up to receive their packs. Meanwhile, I took the opportunity to catch up with a few of the kids, and soon a large crowd gathered for handshaking and sharing of names. Some of the parents and teachers shared their gratitude with me, and of course I didn't know how to tell them how appreciative we were to just have the opportunity to help out.

Indy and I went downstairs to see the girls proudly lined up with their bikes like they were about to start a race. We took some time to say hello to each and every one of them, and hear how old they were, about their school standards, and how far they had to walk to school. Several of them walked up to twelve kilometres round trip. Maxy, Kate and Ally soon joined in. After the customary photos, Indy stood in front of the girls, and flagged them off with a wave of the ChildFund flag. One by one the girls jumped on their bikes, rode off across the courtyard, and out through the gates onto the road. We weren't quite sure what the exact plan was, but the symbolism was nice. Unfortunately, it soon became apparent that some of the young girls hadn't learnt to ride yet. I had to push one along to help her get to the gate, while another didn't know how to stop, and rode off onto the road. Thankfully, there were a lot of people around to stop the traffic, and made sure all of the girls got away safely. I think some riding lessons were in order.

We shared a nice lunch with everyone before heading off in two groups. Bec, Mum, Ally, Maggie and Max headed back to the hotel for a rest, while Nick, Kate, Indy, Gus and I headed to the Chennai Press Club for our second press conference. Gus soon regretted this decision, and the fact that both groups were already on the road didn't stop him from wanting to return to the hotel. He spotted Raju up ahead in traffic, and asked to swap cars. At the next traffic light Nick leaped out of the car with Gus in tow, ran through the traffic, and successfully transferred him to Raju's car. In the meantime, we found out that our driver was following Raju, and was therefore heading in the wrong direction. Don't ask me how. We found the correct directions and at last arrived at the Press Club. Sachal and Done from ChildFund joined us, and once again we shared our story. It took a little to get used to, as the gallery was not particularly responsive, and we were distracted by people coming and going. We were also missing the little master who usually held court, so it wasn't the entertaining show we had put on in the past. After the press conference, Indy had a quick one-on-one interview with a journalist, and then had a short television interview along with Dola and me. In addition to the questions I was usually asked, the journalist wanted to know about how I felt coming to India after the abuse of Indian students in Australia, and if I was worried. It was another one of those questions that I wasn't quite prepared for. I answered as best I could that the racism in Australia was a small element of our country, which unfortunately could be found worldwide. I also made the point that we were in India to represent the many Australians who cared about vulnerable children, and that we always felt welcome and safe when we were here. Kate completed her first press conference, and everyone was very genuine in their responses.

We had a short rest at the hotel before our final send-off dinner with Dola and his team. I wasn't quite sure what Dola had planned, other than that we were heading to a seafood restaurant a little way out of town. Gus and I jumped in the car with Dola, Sachal and Naomi, while our new adopted family member Antony got into the bus with the rest of our crew.

Gus, who had enjoyed an afternoon sleep, was looking very dapper in his Indian shirt with his hair slicked back.

He held court in the car, asking questions and talking with our three friends. He let on that he wanted a jetski motorbike for his birthday, and to take his imaginary friends Oreo and Rainbow Lizard out for a ride. At one point, he tried to hit Dola up for some rupees to help him buy it. He spotted the moon, which was still near full, and we recalled how at the start of the walk it was just a sliver. After a while, Gus piped down, and we continued to drive, and drive, and drive. In the end, the ninety-minute drive took us two and a half hours. It was now nearing 9 pm, and the kids ventured – eyes glazed – from the bus, having fallen asleep along the way. It was worth the drive, however, when we saw we would be eating at an outdoor restaurant right on the beach. Gus immediately ran down to the water, and Bec and I were excited about having an opportunity to kick off our thongs and walk on the sand down to the crashing waves. We stood by the water's edge under the full moon, as a beautiful warm breeze was blowing, and watched Gus hunt the crabs that were scuttling along the sand.

After a while, we rejoined the others to share a beautiful meal of calamari, prawns and fish, and the kids enjoyed non-alcoholic pina coladas. We thanked our new friends – without whom our trip would not have been as memorable. Along with Prem, Esther, and the rest of the team in Bangalore, they had provided us with remarkable support and energy. After dinner, we headed to the beach to chase crabs, and shared in the delightful evening under the full moon. What an incredible end to our time with ChildFund. The kids managed to get a ride in the golf cart that was in the hotel for guests, and were driven the long way back to the car. While waiting, one of the hotel staff came out and very generously gave each of the kids a shell necklace. Fortunately the drive home was a lot quicker as it was past midnight, and the traffic has dissipated. The kids were soon asleep, but I couldn't drift off – my mind was too full. We passed children sleeping on the concrete footpaths by the side of the road, and it was clear that there was still a lot of work to be done.

Day 37
Community visit with KKSS

We awoke to find it stated on the front page of the paper that forty-two per cent of Indian children were malnourished. The story was based on a study commissioned by the prime minister, and incorporated special focus areas such as Odisha and Rajasthan. It highlighted that some progress had been made in recent years, but called for much more work to be done. We, of course, agreed.

We headed out with KKSS. They worked particularly closely with communities living in the Chennai slums. Many of the people were from the nomadic gypsy tribes, and travelled down from northern India to settle in the city. They lived day to day without housing and, as some of the poorest people in India, had little understanding of hygiene, nutrition or education for their children. The tribes came from a life lived as scavengers, nomadically surviving off small animals and birds, and working in very poor-paying jobs such as rag picking. The children unfortunately fell into the category of some of the most vulnerable and deprived children in the world. ChildFund and KKSS helped them to unite as a community, attain basic housing, ensured the kids started going to school, and helped to create new lives. They taught vocational skills such as bead making to ensure more sustainable income options, and enabled the children to start learning instead of working.

Rajini, from the team at KKSS, took us on a visit to one of the local gypsy communities in Pallavaram. The drive took us around an hour and a half through the busy Chennai traffic. We ended up in a semi-rural, semi-urban area, and drove down a small, dirt lane. We jumped out of the van to see the faces of many beautiful children waiting for us, with handmade welcome signs and beaming smiles. As we came to see on our visits, most of the kids seemed to be wearing their best clothes, had henna on their hands, and flowers in their hair, while others were in traditional saris ready to dance. We walked through the mud and rubbish to where the rest of the children were waiting. The first thing that hit us was that the housing was incredibly basic – mainly consisting of thatched-roof huts, surrounding us in an awkward U shape – and that there were people everywhere. Some fifty families lived in the very small area, with many of the single-room houses catering for over eight people. After some very enthusiastic greetings, we dispersed into the crowd. I took a moment to have a quick look around, and couldn't believe the squalor and these kids grew up in. In all my travels through Cambodia, East Timor, Thailand and India, I have found those living conditions to be the most confronting. The houses were incredibly basic. There was just one room, without bedding, and limited cooking facilities – often a hole in the ground with a couple of bricks. There were practically no personal possessions observable, with limited clothing and very few play items. I found the whole scene overwhelming until Gus pulled me into focus, and we worked our way back to the kids. Incredibly, the living conditions represented a significant step up from the conditions they would have otherwise been in. The children, of course, were extremely joyful, and demonstrated an incredible resilience and love for life – regardless of their relative poverty.

We passed a monkey tied up to a nearby post, and headed into a small kindergarten room where more kids were waiting to greet us. We listened to some information about the community, and were then lucky enough to experience some traditional dancing and singing. We even shared a quick rendition of 'Old MacDonald Had a Farm', thanks to Kate's quick thinking. In the meantime, I noticed Maggie was holding a baby boy. She seemed completely at ease, and he was looking up at her with big, brown, trusting eyes. Maggie was a natural with children. They gravitated towards her wherever she went.

Rajini explained that the kids would gladly sing and dance all day if they had the chance. After some time, we thanked everyone for their wonderful performances, and headed outside for some more informal interactions and to see the homes and living conditions of the kids. We were introduced to several children – many of whom were enrolled in the sponsorship program, but not yet linked to a sponsor. We then met a family with six children – one of whom was a beautiful little girl called Mary, who was five years old. Her home was a single room, under a thatched roof, with few of the usual items you would expect to see. There was certainly no fresh food or fruit, no play items, and everything was filthy. While there, I was given the privilege of holding Mary's baby sister for a short time. Of course, I immediately put her into my famous father's cuddle known as the 'jockey' position, with her legs toward me, her head in my hands, and I gently rocked her side to side – a sure-fire guarantee to soothe any baby. I used the position with all three of our kids, and it never failed. The baby would only have been a few weeks old, and was dressed in a filthy jumper but no nappy.

At first meeting I didn't notice anything special about Mary, but as she walked away from us I noticed she was limping, and on closer inspection saw nasty injuries on both legs. One leg had deep scarring, and her other foot was missing three toes. Rajini told us that Mary was involved in a road accident, and had operations on both her legs. I was not sure how successful this had been, as she was clearly still affected. She was also forced to walk on her toes, as one leg was shorter than the other. I hated to think of the pain she would have experienced.

We spent the next hour or so moving from house to house, meeting families and children, and seeing the living conditions firsthand. The slums were much dirtier than others we had visited, with several of the young kids walking around naked, and the older children wearing clothes that looked like they hadn't been washed for some time. Even the way the kids played together was more primitive. There was observable and constant physical play, with firm hitting commonplace – which was again quite unusual and confronting. There was also a noticeable difference in the way the children interacted with us. At some stages it was very intense, with crowds of kids aggressively trying to shake our hands.

On the upside, compared to other communities there were fewer kids working, and more going to school, which was helped by the building of the preschool. The community united around some more profitable income activities, the families were industrious, and their skills were clearly displayed. The teacher at the kindergarten was wonderfully warm and energetic, and many of the parents we saw were interested and involved.

At one point I noticed one little boy crying. On closer inspection, I saw a nasty open and infected wound on his wrist – nothing unusual for young boys. I put the call out to Nurse Ratchet, who quickly created a makeshift triage unit, surrounded by a large group of interested onlookers. Of course once she had treated one patient, many more came looking for help. Bec did her best to provide some preliminary first aid, but it was easy to see how much more could be done with more time, and more resources. She decided to show a couple of the parents what was required to treat the children, and then left all of our medical supplies with them. It was a very confronting day, and the mood was a little sombre on the way back to the hotel. We made a note to discuss with ChildFund how we could direct funds to provide greater assistance to the community, which, later, we were pleased to be able to do by sponsoring five children from the community – and donating extra funds at the completion of our walk.

Day 38
Final leg to Marina Beach, Chennai

After sixteen months of planning and thirty-eight days on the road, we were finally scheduled to walk our final leg from Ambattur to Chennai, and I could not have been more excited. We planned a route that would have us finish at the Gandhi statue on Chennai's Marina Beach – what a fitting end to this incredible adventure. Everyone would be a part of the walk team, with Bec, Mum and Gus joining us closer to the finish line. As we did our final pack up of the walk, Gus grabbed me and asked, 'Are you walking today, Dad? I want to walk today. I am part of the team.' I wasn't sure where it came from, but he definitely was a big part of our team. The whole seventeen-kilometre route would unfortunately be too long for the little man, but I reassured him that he would be joining in later. In recent days he had been telling me, 'I don't want you to go back to work, Daddy.' At three, he already understood the difference between me on leave and me at work. It was another gentle reminder about the incredible value of spending time together.

There had been a massive downpour the night before, so while the sky was bright and shining, the Chennai roads were covered in puddles and mud. After a short drive to Ambattur, we started our walk along the highway in the hot sun, and soon had a quick stop for a roadside coffee. At basically fourteen cents a cup for the delicious drink, it would be hard to go back to buying expensive, and sometimes bad, coffee in Australia.

We made good time down the highway, until we arrived at a major flyover that had wide and busy roads going in every direction, and the only road going the way we wanted wasn't safe to walk on. As a result, we had to cross the other main roads to continue on. Fortunately we all made it in one piece, and rejoined the highway on the other side of the flyover. Our walk route was more interesting, and more difficult, than usual, as there were many turns along the way, and we only had my makeshift map. The highway took us into urban Chennai, and after around seventy-five minutes, we arrived at our first turn off the main road. I gave Bec a call, who wasn't far away, and who thought she would easily be able to find us, given she had a copy of our route. We took a couple more turns, and all of a sudden found ourselves on an unknown road. Not only had we lost our way, but Bec wouldn't be able to find us. The kids sat by the side of the road with Nick, Kate, and a packet of chips, and I backtracked our steps in an attempt to rendezvous. After a few frustrating minutes, I could see the bus approaching, and we were together again at last.

We drove back to meet the team, and with some updated directions from Raju, were back on the right path. Gus decided he was ready to be on the team too, so eight kilometres out from our destination, I had the little man on my shoulders enjoying a packet of chips and a mango juice, and hoped my back could hold up for the duration of the walk. Raju drove up ahead with Mum, and we continued on our walk toward Marina Beach. Mum jumped out of the van when we were three and a half kilometres from our destination, and the full team was together for the final dash to the finishing line. We had to cross a few major roads, but by that stage we were reading the Indian traffic well, and managed it unscathed. Well, almost unscathed. Nick nearly got himself arrested after filming on a section of road where it was prohibited. After one look from a very serious police officer, the camera was put away.

Indy was the first to spot the top of the Gandhi statue as we walked down the main road to the marina. The kids had been fantastic all day, and were very excited. Knowing that they were on the final walk of the trip meant they could relax and get the job done. By that stage my shoulders and back were aching, and I was covered in sweat, but it meant a lot to have Gus with us. We left the west coast of India together, and we were all there heading to the finish line on the east coast. As we walked toward the statue, we could see our very friendly film crew manager, Sonu Kumar, who had made a special personal trip to meet us at the beach. It wasn't in his brief, but I think by that stage he felt like such a part of the team that he wanted to be there at the finish – and we were very excited to see him. One more main road to cross and we made it under the watchful eye of Gandhi, our major inspiration.

We gathered around the statue until one by one the kids took off toward the beach. The water was at least 750 metres away, so all we could see were the backs of our four kids and the ocean off in the distance. Gus decided this was a great idea, so he and I took off in hot pursuit. We passed all of the stalls on the beach, and saw the kids standing at the edge of the slightly brown water. They desperately wanted to swim to commemorate the end of their walk, but I think they could still recall Antony's advice that the water was not clean enough to do so – and this meant a lot coming from the man who once said that a bit of bacteria is good for you. The kids may have been smart enough to listen, but not me. Gus and I took off our shoes, and I was filled with emotion and the desperate need to hit the water. I ran at full pace past the kids, and leapt into the waves fully dressed to celebrate the end of our massive adventure. Trying my best not to swallow, I glided under the warm Chennai water for some time. All of the effort that had gone into the trip was channelled into that one dive. It was an incredible feeling, clothes and all.

As you can imagine this was too much for the kids who needed no further encouragement. They were told to keep their heads above water – not like me! We linked arms, and jumped up and down, celebrating our achievement together. Gus and Bec soon joined, but Mum thought better of it. I wondered if my 'Jim Courier' moment would come back to haunt me in later days. Jim Courier, after winning the Australian Open, jumped into the Yarra River in Melbourne, only to get quite sick afterwards.

After a while in the water, we all came up on the sand, and took a shot of our feet in a circle around the Coast to Coast logo Kate had drawn on the sand. As we were doing so, a poor young girl from the local beachside slum grabbed me by the arm and begged for some money. It was a sign that while this adventure had been incredible and was nearing an end, there was far more work to be done.

We made the long walk back up the beach to the Gandhi statue for a few special photos, and some well-earned moments of reflection. Sonu thanked us for what we had done for his country, and we thanked him for what his country had done for us. Indy, Bec and I shared a few special words before the five of us had a family hug. We thought back to eighteen months ago when we first had this crazy idea. I grabbed Maxy, reminded him of what he had just done, and told him that if he could walk across India at ten, he could do anything.

As I reflected on our journey, I gave particular thought to the goals we set for ourselves as a family. We set about to raise funds and awareness of the needs of vulnerable children, to experience the wonder of giving, and to travel together as a family. Sixteen months in the planning, thirty-eight days traversing over 1000 kilometres – walking over 600 kilometres with five children – over A$60,000 raised for ChildFund India, and over seventy articles in Indian papers and online. What an incredible team effort.

Day 39
With thanks

It was our final day in India. Bec and Indy were packing their bags while Maggie and Gus ran around with their cousins. We had eaten breakfast, and were planning for a quiet day to ready ourselves for the long trip home. The girls were heading out to get henna on their hands and feet, and Mum was getting her last fix of Gus before we parted ways for our different home cities.

I took a minute to think about the people who contributed to our walk: Di, Rachel and all of the team at ChildFund Australia who were with us every step of the way; Dola, Naomi, Antony, Prem, Abdul, Esther, and ChildFund India; Kiriya Pushpa; Grama Vikas and KKSS who went out of their way to provide a very special experience. We will never forget the support you provided us.

To all the people who donated their hard-earned funds, a very big and special thank you. We were able to see the difference your donations made firsthand. So many people were incredibly generous, and we were appreciative of every dollar donated. The words of encouragement posted via Facebook, email and our blog gave us the motivation and energy to push forward – particularly on the long and lonely days when we felt a million miles from home.

Finally to our walk team. Firstly to Nicola and Eibhlin who were just amazing. You came to India with such an incredible attitude, and provided us with so much positive energy and practical support. You were dearly missed after you left, and we thought of you often on the trip.

To my sister Kate, and Ally and Max – you did an inspirational job on your first trip to India, and I hope that you took an unforgettable life experience with you. With limited time and funds we were so appreciative that you made this trip a priority for your family; it wouldn't have been the same without you. Picking you up from the airport still remains one of the most special times on our trip.

Mum and Nick were there every step of the way, and both, in their own way, provided a crucial level of support to the team. We saw a new side to you even after all of our time together, and I think you surprised even yourselves with your efforts – particularly leading up to the walk. Again I hope the experience was one you will never forget.

Bec. You are an amazing woman, and I don't know how you managed to do it, but with each challenge you found a new depth to your strength and resilience. You managed the kids and me while preparing for, and ultimately completing the trip, and I don't know how you did it. We were so lucky to have you, and promise not to take you for granted. To Indy, Maggie and Gus. You are our best friends, and we felt so grateful that you were prepared to join with us on these adventures. You made a massive contribution to our collective experience every day, and in your own way each of you demonstrated just how beautiful, resilient and strong you are. I couldn't be more proud of you all.

My final words are for the children of India. You are the reason we planned and executed our journey. You welcomed us into your villages, homes and lives with a spirit of generosity and humility. We felt so privileged to have had this wonderful opportunity to spend time with each of you, and want to thank you for providing us with the opportunity to make a small contribution to supporting you, and ensuring that your childhood was safe, healthy, and full of learning and possibilities.

We were the Coast to Coast team and we had just walked across India.

Afterword

The Big Question: is it safe?

It was late November, and a matter of weeks before we left for India. We were attending the book launch of the powerful *Memoirs of a Suburban Girl* by our good friend, Deb Kandelaars. At the launch afterparty – a first for Bec and me – we enjoyed speaking to friends from our old hometown of Middleton; the topic of conversation was our upcoming trip. As usual, the initial reaction was, 'Wow that sounds amazing,' closely followed by, 'Are you guys crazy?' After some discussion about the trip, my friend – a father to two kids, who lived a pretty settled and safe life on the Fleurieu Peninsula – turned to me and asked, 'Is it safe?' I rabbitted on with some half answer for a while, and then ended up saying, 'I don't actually know, is anything really safe?' I then went and stewed on this question for the next few weeks and, honestly, every day we were away.

The truth is there is often that little voice in your head telling you to play it safe, to stay in your comfort zone. My voice didn't need encouragement; I had tried to pull out on several occasions. Of course Bec would just say, 'Don't be stupid, we are doing it.' I guess it was like anything in life – there are always risks. You can't really avoid them, you can only choose how to manage them. As we planned for the trip, we asked ourselves about the risk of going, but also about the risk of not going. What was the risk of allowing our kids to grow up without the broader perspective of life lived in other countries and cultures and, more importantly, knowing what life was like for the deprived, vulnerable and excluded kids? What was the risk of not showing our kids that they, too, could set big hairy audacious goals and then achieve them?

I would never forget our new friend Paul Hameister, the sixty-eighth Australian to summit Mount Everest. He told of his passage up the mountain, and a particular section called the Death Zone. He recalled that it wasn't his death zone. His death zone was sitting at home on the couch watching television. I could relate to this, I knew it would be easy for us as a family to get stuck living our lives in safe little boxes, worrying about mortgages and schedules and work and school, and forgetting about our dreams and the world of possibilities out there.

Over the sixteen months leading up to the walk, our family lived with an absolute sense of purpose. We made the decision to go on the adventure, planned our trip, gave talks at local community groups and schools, conducted fundraising events, and learned about the needs of vulnerable children, all before we took a step. We then travelled to India, spent every day together for six weeks, turned off our phones and emails, and most importantly, met thousands of inspirational Indian kids and families. Our kids made so many new friends, and provided important items to improve the health, safety and education of others. They learnt about sponsorship, and community and child development. They had a wealth of new experiences that will carry them through their life. And perhaps, most importantly, they knew they could dream big – even something that they could not see or understand – and set about and achieve these dreams.

I wonder what it must feel like at nine or thirteen to be able to say I walked across India.

Travelling as a family meant managing risks. It meant partnering with a wonderful organisation like ChildFund, who provided enormous support. It meant securing the services of a car and driver for the trip, to enable the kids to make a choice every day about whether they wanted to walk. It meant securing accommodation in advance, and not moving on a daily basis, to enable sufficient rest time between stops. It meant enforcing this rest time within the trip, to ensure everyone could recover. It meant making decisions on a couple of occasions not to walk, as the roads weren't safe. It meant mixing up the accommodation, so the kids could experience very basic accommodation, through to a couple of smarter hotels. They were the various ways we chose to manage the risks, and complete the trip in a way that we considered safe for our family.

Having completed our walk safely and with good health, I was so happy for our family, but also for others who I know had been watching and starting to think about what they can do with their families. Life is there to be lived. Bec and I strongly believed in providing our kids with unforgettable life experiences, and spending time with them while they were young.

There were risks in doing and there were risks in not doing. Our regrets in life are rarely based on what we have done, but more in what we have chosen not to do. So what choice do you have to make? We were already starting to plan our next adventure as a family, and couldn't wait to see what else we could achieve.

Europe @ 2.4 km/h

Ken Haley

Europe was the first continent to win a name for itself, and is the smallest of them all. So it should be easy to comprehend and its people should share a common outlook, right? Wrong.

In his second book, wheelchair traveller Ken Haley crosses the Continent the long way round – from Russia to Portugal via the Arctic – and finds that Europeans are an endangered species.

At the stately pace of 2.4 km/h the author is not out to break too many speed records, and takes comfort in the self-delusion that the slower he goes, the more he sees.

While searching for true Europeans, Haley is embroiled in adventures that range from sharing a house with bank robbers in Norway to taking on the house at Monte Carlo. He also turns detective and discovers unsettling truths about his own European family.

From the Arctic in summer to the Mediterranean in winter, Haley is always pushing against the grain, but his reward lies in meeting some of the most distinctive, charming and outrageous characters imaginable.

By turns funny, serious, whimsical and witty, Haley's account of the Europeans, a people who seem to think Europe is somewhere else, will lead you on a twelve-nation tour de force – covering 26,000 km by train, bus, plane and ship – into the heart of Europe.

ISBN 978 1 86254 917 3

for more information please visit www.wakefieldpress.com.au

From Burma to Myanmar

On the road to Mandalay

Lydia Laube

What a ride! In a death-defying taxi with no windows, I was flown along the roads in a howling gale. Horrible. I sat directly behind the driver hoping he would act as an air bag when the inevitable collision came. In that position I couldn't see the worst that was happening around us, like pedestrians peeling off our fenders.

Lydia Laube is no stranger to near-death experiences. She encounters many on the five journeys she takes to discover Myanmar, or Burma as it was known on the first three of these.

As ever Lydia chooses the route less travelled to reach and explore this wondrous land of pagodas and paddy fields. Under Myanmar's magic spell, she pays homage to the world's biggest python, visits the world's largest book and falls in love with a little horse called Madonna.

From Burma to Myanmar is Lydia Laube's ninth travel book. Her first, *Behind the Veil*, was published in 1991. It has been an Australian bestseller, reprinted eleven times and translated and republished in five other countries.

ISBN 978 1 74305 392 8

for more information please visit www.wakefieldpress.com.au

For the Love of Rhinos (and this life)

Heather Caddick

As a child Heather Caddick studied clouds, seeing a world of possibilities unfolding in their ghostly shapes, like mirages. This collection of stories spans a forty-year compulsion to reach the next mirage, whether on horseback to Maree droving 500 head of cattle, or sharing a picnic rug with a curious Savannah baboon and his family in the Fantale Crater in Ethiopia.

Heather's stories, both enlightening and entertaining, carry a message – we must hold on to our wonder in this precious planet, and the wildlife that remains wild, learning to protect it for the sake of our children's children.

ISBN 978 1 74305 353 9

Those Dry-stone Walls

Stories from South Australia's Stone Age

Bruce Munday and Kristin Munday

Beautiful stone was nature's gift to South Australia, and an irresistible building material for early settlers. Many stone walls, without mortar or with no more than mud as glue, have defied gravity and the elements all these years. Or did gravity combine with deft balance to sustain them?

Join Bruce and Kristin Munday as they traverse South Australia in search of these walls, finding historic masterpieces and insights into rural life in the years following settlement. *Those Dry-stone Walls* is rich with beautiful imagery of these walls, the stories behind them, and advice to inspire you to follow in the footsteps of our early settlers and start building your own.

ISBN 978 1 74305 125 2

for more information please visit www.wakefieldpress.com.au

Never Carry Your Own Briefcase

John M. Allgrove

On arrival on the footpath in front of the hotel, with French driver holding the door open for the PM – I had already ascertained which side he wished to travel – Prime Minister Fraser turned to me and said, 'I want to go in that car,' pointing to a stretched limousine parked some fifty metres away to the right. It happened to be the French press vehicle!

Never Carry Your Own Briefcase is the always personal, often humorous story of a much-travelled Australian Trade Commissioner. In a career spanning more than thirty-four years, John Allgrove's assignments took him to Calcutta, Bombay, Athens, Cairo, Hong Kong, Taipei, Bangkok, Paris, Jakarta, Seoul and Frankfurt, before he retired after his final posting in Singapore in 1995. His children were born in Hong Kong, Taipei, Bangkok and Paris.

Austrade's mission is to increase the international success of Australian business. *Never Carry Your Own Briefcase* gives us a unique glimpse into Austrade's endeavours over decades, via the on-the-ground experiences of one of its longest-serving officers.

ISBN 978 1 74305 366 9

for more information please visit www.wakefieldpress.com.au

Once Upon a Distant Journey

Hendrik Gout

What would it be like if your bike didn't need a number plate and you didn't need a licence? Why not vote toll roads into extinction? Should we ban random breath testing and use simulators instead? Hendrik answers all these questions.

These yarns take you on journeys across Australia from the outback to the sea. We feel for ourselves the relationship between man and motorbike, between humanity and nature, between people who love each other – and those met only fleetingly.

Hendrik takes us down roads packed with beauty and delight and others with obstacles and surprises. His quirky sense of humour and intimate knowledge of this Wide Brown Land offers fresh ways of identifying with the country, its history, its people, geography, and uniquely Australian culture.

This is a travel book with wisdom which captures the essence of Australia. Voices of ordinary and extraordinary Australians speak to us directly with honesty and candour.

Hendrik shares experiences that could be had only on a motorbike. An enormously satisfying read: the thrills, spills and joys that exist for all of us between road and sky – whether we ride or not.

No finer traveller's tale has ere been told. – Homer

Makes The Motorcycle Dairies read like a fairy story. – Che Guevara

I wish I'd seen as much of Australia as Hendrik has.
– Matthew Flinders

Had Hendrik written about my journey to Cathay, I may well have become famous. – Marco Polo

ISBN 978 1 74305 334 8

for more information please visit www.wakefieldpress.com.au

Dark Dreams

Australian refugee stories by young writers aged 11–20 years

Sonja Dechian, Heather Millar and Eva Sallis (eds)

Dark Dreams: Australian refugee stories is a unique anthology of essays, interviews, and stories written by children and young adults. The stories are the finest of hundreds collected through a nationwide schools competition in 2002. The essays and stories represent many different countries and themes. Some focus on survival, some on horrors, some on the experiences and alienation of a new world. This book will have a key role to play in schools across Australia.

ISBN 978 1 86254 629 5

for more information please visit www.wakefieldpress.com.au

No Place Like Home

Australian stories by young writers aged 8–21 years

Sonja Dechian, Jenni Devereaux, Heather Millar and Eva Sallis (eds)

Following the success of *Dark Dreams: Australian refugee stories*, this extraordinary collection of stories creates a narrative picture of Australians, past and present. It is also a mosaic of journeys, for we are all displaced peoples or the descendents of displaced peoples, whether we are from Indigenous, settler, migrant or refugee families.

ISBN 978 1 86254 686 8

for more information please visit www.wakefieldpress.com.au

Wakefield Press is an independent publishing and distribution company based in Adelaide, South Australia. We love good stories and publish beautiful books. To see our full range of books, please visit our website at www.wakefieldpress.com.au where all titles are available for purchase.

Find us!

Twitter: www.twitter.com/wakefieldpress
Facebook: www.facebook.com/wakefield.press
Instagram: instagram.com/wakefieldpress